How *Not* to Get Published

Claire Gillman

Claire Gillman has been a professional writer for more than 25 years. In that time, she has written 23 non-fiction and creative-fiction books for adults and children. Her most recent titles include *Make Money from Freelance Writing* (Hodder 2012) and *Write Fantastic Non-Fiction and Get Published* (Hodder 2011).

Claire was the editor of several women's consumer magazines before changing tack to become a regular freelance contributor to many leading magazines and national newspapers, most notably the *Guardian* and *The Times*.

Claire is also an editor for The Writers' Workshop, regularly writing critiques and discussing manuscripts to help writers towards publication. She also leads writers' workshops and writing groups in various locations, always with the emphasis on fun, style, relaxation and discovering inner creativity.

Teach® Yourself

How *Not* to Get Published

Claire Gillman

First published in Great Britain in 2013 by Hodder & Stoughton. An Hachette UK company.

First published in US in 2013 by The McGraw-Hill Companies, Inc.

British Library Cataloguing in Publication Data: a catalogue record for this title is available from the British Library.

Library of Congress Catalog Card Number: on file.

10 9 8 7 6 5 4 3 2 1

Typeset by Cenveo® Publisher Services.

Printed and bound in Great Britain by CPI Group (UK) Ltd, Croydon CR0 4YY.

Hodder & Stoughton policy is to use papers that are natural, renewable and recyclable products and made from wood grown in sustainable forests. The logging and manufacturing processes are expected to conform to the environmental regulations of the country of origin.

Hodder & Stoughton Ltd
338 Euston Road
London NW1 3BH
www.hodder.co.uk

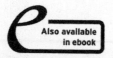

Acknowledgements

Warm thanks and appreciation to my agent, Chelsey Fox, and editors, Victoria Roddam and Sam Richardson. I also owe a huge debt of gratitude to all those who contributed their wisdom and professional experiences in the form of case studies, and to all the writers and students who have inspired me and taught me over the years.

Finally, I would like to acknowledge the courage of all those new writers who are about to take the plunge and commit their words to print – good luck with your future writing projects and I hope that you experience the joy of becoming a published author.

Contents

1

Why write?

In this chapter you will learn:

- ▶ *That there are common traps that can trip up the unwary writer*
- ▶ *How writing can be an integral and rewarding part of your life*
- ▶ *How this book can help you*
- ▶ *What's in it for you, the writer.*

The very fact that you are reading the opening pages of this book suggests that you have a passion for writing, a message that you wish to share with a wider audience and/or a desire to see a writing project in print. And I am delighted to hear it because I love writing. Yes, it can be fun and fulfilling, yet frustrating and challenging in equal measure, but it is always interesting.

What draws us to write is different for each individual and yet there are also common bonds that bind writers. Often, there is a love of language – just playing with words and how they fit together can be a joy in itself. For many, it is simply the best form of self-expression, and writing down thoughts and feelings can bring meaning and clarity to your ideas or to a situation. For those of you who have specialist knowledge or who have undergone remarkable experiences, what better way to share your gifts with a wider audience than through the written word?

The desire to write, then, is shared, and, irrespective of the genre of book you have chosen, it behoves us all to produce the very best writing for our readers that we can. And herein lies the problem. The enthusiasm and intention of novice writers is undeniable, but there are many common pitfalls and mistakes that can befall the inexperienced writer and, sadly, these often result in a manuscript being rejected by prospective publishers. The aim of this book is to identify these pitfalls and to point out how they can easily be avoided once you know about them, so increasing the chances that your submission for publication will be successful.

In case you are wondering how I am equipped to help you with your quest, let me share a little bit about myself. I have been writing professionally for nearly 30 years and I love what I do and the fact that I am still learning. In that time, I have interviewed some amazing people and I have written about subjects that I have found fascinating – and I hope the resulting features/books have inspired a similar response in my readers.

As a staff journalist, I have edited consumer magazines specializing in health, parenting, travel and spiritual living – all of which are subjects close to my heart – and I am currently the co-editor of *Kindred Spirit* magazine. As a freelancer, I have contributed to women's magazines and national newspapers.

I have written over a dozen non-fiction books for adults and a series of creative non-fiction titles for children under the pen name Rory Storm.

I am also a workshop leader and an editor for the writing consultancy The Writers' Workshop, specializing in non-fiction and life writing. It is hugely rewarding to be able to help new writers to get their ideas and writing into shape for possible publication. Over the years, I have seen many of the same writing blunders cropping up time and time again in the manuscripts I receive, and I share them here with you in the pages of this book so that you are forewarned and forearmed, and thus able to avoid making the same mistakes.

By seeking some help at the early stages of your writing project, you are ahead of the game and, if you follow the advice contained in these pages, you should be able to polish and finesse your writing and its presentation, so that you can get it to a much better standard before submission.

Remember this: Increase your chances from the outset

Inexperienced writers often make the same mistakes that curtail any chance of their manuscript being accepted for publication. Once these errors are ironed out, or avoided from the outset, the odds of acceptance are increased tenfold.

'Writers are born, not made'

Like most axioms, there is a modicum of truth in the above statement, but it is not wholly accurate. The desire to write despite all the obstacles that will be put in your way – the pressures of daily living and the inevitable rejections that are a part of every writer's life – is something that cannot be manufactured, admittedly. You have to want to write quite badly, have a passion for it even, because it can be hard work and getting your book published will not be easy. However, *How* Not *to Get Published* is designed to give you some insider knowledge of the publishing world that will help you through the submission process and signpost some of the wrong turnings that you should avoid when writing. It offers short cuts that you might miss if you were travelling the writer's path alone.

The very fact that you have a desire to improve and are willing to seek help suggests that you are already on the way to becoming a better writer. You could probably find out a great deal of the information contained within these pages for yourself through trial and error but that would be time-consuming and discouraging. This book will save you time and help you to circumvent the more common pitfalls, so that you can concentrate on perfecting your style and honing your skills.

How this book can help

Throughout these pages I draw on my own experiences and my conversations (formal and informal) with my students and those I mentor in their writing careers to find inspiration for what to include. There are some practical exercises (labelled 'Try it now') that you can try which are designed to engender greater confidence in your abilities and to get you on the first rung of the publishing ladder. Some you will tackle happily and willingly, I am sure; others, however, will pose more of a challenge and take you outside your comfort zone. None is compulsory but all will be beneficial if attempted.

There are tactics, strategies and useful information ('Writers' top tips') plus aide-memoire boxes (labelled 'Remember this') in every chapter that will nudge you in the right direction and help you to remember the most salient points. And in the 'Case study' boxes there is also advice from professionals and experts in their field of publishing, which I hope you will find interesting and insightful.

The key points of each chapter are summed up in 'Focus points' at the end of the chapter, so that you have the information in a nutshell if you are pressed for time.

Whether you choose to cherry-pick the sections that resonate with you, go straight to the chapter that is most pertinent to the current stage of your writing project, or read this book from start to finish, all are fine. Simply find the path that is best for you and your writing.

What about you?

As you have decided to enlist some help from this book, I am guessing that you probably have your heart set on a writing project that you would like to see through to fruition, but you perhaps doubt your abilities or that you have the talent to finish a book. This self-doubt is common to nearly every writer I know, even the most successful. You are far from alone in your insecurity. Even so, it is probably one of the reasons that you have put off writing your book until now. But, despite your misgivings, if you have the desire to write, then you have to take the plunge and get started. (There are tips for beating procrastination in Chapter 2.)

Whether you want to write a novel, a non-fiction guide, a play or a screenplay, you must devote time and effort to the process if you are going to produce something that an agent or publisher will consider for publication. You may decide that you want to keep your writing as a pleasurable but serious hobby and that getting something into print would be the icing on the cake. Perhaps you want to write as a sideline – a second income stream to your main career. Or possibly writing for a living has been a lifelong ambition and this attempt at getting published is your first toe in the water. Whichever applies to you, you must set aside some time for writing.

Undoubtedly, we all lead busy lives, and this probably means sacrificing something else (surfing the Web, a favourite television show, drinks after work, or keeping up with Facebook friends), but the truth is that, if you want to be published, you have to be disciplined in devoting part of your day or week to your writing project. It does not have to be a long stretch of time, but regularity is what counts when it comes to getting the best out of your writing.

Remember this: Writing is totally non-discriminatory

You can write at any age, and in any language. You can be fit or unhealthy, fat or slim, attractive or pug-ugly, supremely well qualified or ill educated... None of this matters – to be a writer, all you have to have is something to say.

As with many things, regular practice is the best way to improve, and, in the case of writing, it is the most efficient way of hitting your groove and getting into the flow. In my experience, a regular half an hour is much more productive than an occasional four-hour marathon.

While it is essential to make the time to write, it is also helpful and desirable to have some dedicated space for writing, but it is not a necessity. With the advent of modern technology, you can actually write pretty much anywhere at any time. As a professional writer, I use a home office, but you can choose to sit in your favourite armchair with your laptop, or even in a Wi-Fi-enabled café or library, if that is what works best for you.

However, do not let this easy access to the tools of the trade lull you into a false sense of security. Although it is easy to dash off a chapter on a computer, and it will look neat and professional, the quality of your writing is what counts. The facility to use PC editing tools such as cut and paste and track changes, among others, can dupe the unwary into thinking that they are self-editing their work, when in fact they are simply moving bad prose from one place to another. It is wonderful that more and more people are writing because the physical effort of producing a book is less arduous, but quality control is still needed if your book is to impress an audience.

Try it now: Get in touch with other writers

Staying the course and getting your project finished is one of the hardest challenges facing the novice writer. Of course, you will have me by your side offering advice and support, but writing can be an isolating experience. The good news is that there are lots of budding authors out there. So why not look online or go to the library and track down some local writing groups? Get in touch to see whether they are appropriate for you, and then join in.

Whatever your reasons for writing and whichever method you choose to achieve your goals, I encourage you to be enthusiastic about it, to take your writing seriously while enjoying the process, and to hone your skills so that you can produce the best piece of writing for you, your reader and for any potential agents or publishers.

Case study: Jonathan Telfer, editor of *Writing Magazine* and *Writers' News*

'I think most of us feel like we were born writers and for the most part that's where we get the drive to keep at it in the face of rejection. Among *Writing Magazine* readers it seems to be that passion, rather than anything else, that motivates them to write, which isn't to say that nobody expects any payment for it.

'Even those who write out of passion and a pure love of writing want to get published. The search for validation drives a lot of us, as in "Someone somewhere thinks my work is good enough to print." There are people who want nothing more than to write for themselves and never show their work to anyone, but the majority, even of those who are doing it purely for the love of writing, are at some stage going to want to take it to an audience, to find readers for it or hopefully, even better, to sell it to a publisher or put it on Amazon themselves.

'It's a fabulous time to be a writer in some ways, but in others it's more difficult than ever. The number of books being published keeps escalating, so it's more difficult to make your mark and it's more difficult to get accepted, but, on the other hand, doing it yourself has never been easier. For those writers who are planning to do it themselves, we've now got past a lot of the stigma of self-publishing, so the returns can be higher, and possibly better than they might be by getting published traditionally. So, it's a trying time for writers trying to keep on top of all these things, but, if you want to make a go of it, the opportunities are definitely there.

'The problem is, of course, that it's easier for *anyone* to get a book out there, whether self-published, Amazon or e-book. The marketplace is growing so fast that it's more and more difficult to make yourself heard above the clamour.

'I'm very lucky to get paid to write and edit. My entire life I have always loved words — shuffling them, juggling them and playing with them, so to be able to do that all day and every day hardly feels like work. It can be a lovely way to earn some extra money if it's not your day job and, if you are lucky enough to support yourself with writing eventually, even better.

Focus points

- ✲ Most writers have a passion to share their ideas and/or knowledge and to have their voice heard – and that is all that is needed.
- ✲ Inexperience can lead to common writing mistakes, but these can be avoided with a little insider know-how.
- ✲ Irrespective of the kind of book you want to write, there are certain pitfalls to avoid that are common to all genres.
- ✲ You can write anywhere at any time of the day or night, but devoting dedicated time to your writing is essential if you are to succeed.

Next step

You may well feel that you should really have got down to writing long ago, but there's no time like the present. In the next chapter we'll look at ways to cure procrastination and to get you started.

2

Getting started

In this chapter you will learn:

▶ *How to beat procrastination*
▶ *How to avoid over-planning and over-researching your project*
▶ *How to identify and overcome your fears*
▶ *Short cuts to getting started.*

How many times have you told your friends and acquaintances that you are writing a book or a script when, in reality, you have yet to put pen to paper (or fingers to keyboard, to be more accurate in this technological age)? In your head, you are telling the truth because you desperately want to write, you have set yourself the goal of writing and you even have the concept/idea planned out, but the reality is that starting such a momentous and personally important project is simply overwhelming.

Even professional writers are guilty of putting off the inevitable moment when they should start an assignment – and remember, they don't get paid if they don't deliver. Many of my colleagues use the excuse that 'they work better to a deadline' and so leave starting to write until the eleventh hour. In fact, I'm guilty of using that hoary old chestnut myself. But the truth of the matter is that, for many writers – professionals and enthusiasts alike – it is simply an excuse to delay the fateful moment when you commit your first sentences to print.

Writers' top tip 1: If not now, when?

There is no time like the present to physically start the process of writing. Delaying for a more auspicious start time or date is simply a delaying tactic. The teachers' favourite tag 'If not now, when?' is very apt here.

So, let's make it official, shall we? The very first common pitfall that most writers fall into is that they delay starting to write. And the first and perhaps most important tip of this book is that there is no right time to start writing. I have known writers who have planned to start their book/article on one particular day but something unexpected and unforeseen takes the morning and they convince themselves that there is no point in starting in the afternoon, and so another day is lost. Similarly, how many writers, when planning to start their project, decide that Wednesday is an odd day to start on so postpone until the following Monday, at the start of a fresh week? Does any of this sound familiar?

If so, don't beat yourself up. It is human nature to put off the things that we dislike as well as the things that matter enormously to us – and your writing project probably falls into the latter category. So what can be done?

First, let's identify the main ways in which we procrastinate and then we can look at ways to overcome these self-made obstacles.

Procrastination

Sometimes we recognize that we are procrastinating and we know why. However, the mind can play clever and deceptive tricks on us, so there are also occasions when we genuinely believe that there are obstacles to starting a new writing project that actually are manufactured by our devious minds to prevent us from getting going.

Conscious procrastination is easy to defeat and later in this chapter we'll have some useful tips for putting a halt to these blatant delaying tactics. The subconscious procrastination is harder to conquer as it is often rooted in our deep-seated inner fears – fear of failure, fear of rejection, fear of success (strange but true), fear of revealing your true self … the list is scarily long.

The best way to overcome these subconscious fears is to recognize that they may exist and to face them head on. As Franklin D. Roosevelt famously said in his inaugural address in 1933, 'So, first of all, let me assert my firm belief that the only thing we have to fear is fear itself…'

It's worth asking yourself a few frank, soul-searching questions. Do I really want to write? Is it actually a long-held ambition or something that I have told others I am doing so I cannot back out? Why haven't I started? Why am I delaying? Listen carefully and intuitively to the answers. Perhaps acknowledging that you would rather live with the dream of being a successful writer than have a go and potentially have your dream shattered is the first step to recognizing that you, and you alone, are holding yourself back. Perhaps you will come up with another reason but, whatever your answers, if they are honest, they will help you to move forward, whether that means starting or shelving the project without self-recriminations.

However, what you will most likely learn from this self-scrutiny is the fact that writing means a great deal to you. So, if you actually make a commitment to it and get started, you may find that you have a real talent, or you may discover that the whole process is simply therapeutic and/or fun even. Who knows how the experience of writing will affect you ... until you try.

So let's face up to the many fears that stop you and countless other writers from enjoying their art, and then we can press on.

FEAR OF FAILURE

If you are a keen fan of literature, you may find you have been comparing yourself with your favourite authors and, in all probability, you feel sure that you cannot measure up. Thinking that your work will not be good enough is possibly the most common reason for would-be writers to give up before they even start. However, your writing does not have to be a work of literary genius to be of merit and to be valued by your readers.

Some of the most powerful manuscripts I have read in my role as a critiquing editor for The Writers' Workshop have been life-writing projects, where the author has had a life-changing experience and has felt the need to share their discoveries with others who may find themselves in similar circumstances. They are not necessarily the best-crafted and best-honed prose I've read, but often they've been the most arresting and affecting. And many of them have gone on to find a publisher.

Whether you're looking at writing a non-fiction book to share your passion for a subject, to tell a personal story or to share an original idea in a novel, no one else can tell the story the way it plays out in your head. Share your wisdom and your creativity and you could help and inspire thousands of people.

And don't judge yourself on the half-finished product either. We are all our own harshest critics, and, although finding your writing wanting when you are only halfway through the project may be entirely natural, it is not wise to give up – you are judging it too soon. Keep in mind that this is not the fully rounded, polished product – so don't quit just yet.

Writers' top tip 2: Forget peers and posterity

Don't worry about how your peers or posterity will judge your work – no one can possibly predict this. You might as well give it a go.

FEAR OF FINISHING

The last paragraph neatly segues with the next 'common fear', namely the fear of finishing. So many writers cherish an idea for so long and perfect it in their mind's eye, but when they start, the reality does not live up to the ideal. So, rather than finishing the writing project, they leave their half-finished, imperfect creation and move on to the next idea, which, needless to say, is perfect in their imagination.

If you fall into this trap, which is an extension of fear of failure, then I would simply say give your project and yourself a chance. When you finish, you can go back and finesse your work and, who knows, you may surprise yourself with just how good it is.

As a professional writer, I find I am more pleased with some projects than others. Some articles or books are laborious to write and others flow. That's a fact of freelance life. When you finish one project, you move on to the next. Months later, the book proofs or the finished publication arrive on your desk. And sometimes, I confess, I reread the piece and I'm pleasantly surprised. So don't judge yourself too harshly too early in the writing process. Finish it and, if necessary, put it away for a while. When you return to it with fresh eyes, you may well be in for a nice surprise too.

FEAR OF REJECTION

This is a common fear in all walks of life but is especially relevant to the writer. The simple truth is that it takes courage to share your creativity with the wider world and all writers face rejection at some point in their careers. It is unavoidable. It is better to find positive ways to handle the rejection than to avoid it by not writing at all.

The most famous example of a successful writer who faced rejection is J.K. Rowling. It is claimed that she received 12 rejections before her book was signed. Rowling will not confirm the exact number (who can blame her?), preferring to leave the final number of rejections at 'a lot'. She is the author most often cited in discussions on writer rejections because of the phenomenal success of the Harry Potter series, but very few writers can say that they have never had an idea or a feature/manuscript turned down.

So, if you are writing in the hope of being published, you must prepare yourself for the fact that your work may not be taken up by the first editor, agent or publisher to whom you send it. You just hope that it will find success with the next approach. This may sound trite, but it really is that simple. If you want to write for an audience, you are opening yourself to criticism and rejection – but what I will say is this: it's well worth it to see your work in print. I won't pretend that it doesn't hurt to receive a rejection – of course it does, and it's impossible to inure yourself to all criticism –but you do get over it. So don't let fear of rejection stop you from realizing your writing ambitions.

Writers' top tip 3: Take criticism on board

When publishers give a reason in their rejection letters, sometimes a pattern emerges. In that case, you can take this message on board and amend/improve your manuscript accordingly. In this way, you are turning what could be seen as a negative into a positive because your manuscript is stronger as a result of those rejections.

FEAR OF SUCCESS

This is an odd one to include, you may think, but it is a fact that some writers are afraid that, if their writing takes off and is successful, it will change their lives irrevocably. Fame and fortune do not appeal to those who fear they may lose old friends, familiar comforts and their anonymity to the new lifestyle of publishing success.

Yet writers belong to one of the few categories where public acclaim and financial reward do not necessarily have to plunge you into the spotlight. There are plenty of blockbuster authors who remain anonymous and who can pass in the street without being recognized. And you can always dispose of your new-found wealth in a compassionate and responsible way if you do not like being rich.

FEAR OF REVEALING YOUR TRUE SELF

One of the hardest things about showing your writing to someone else is that, not only are you opening yourself to criticism, but, if your writing is personal, then you are also baring your soul to them. Even if it is a work of fiction rather than a personal memoir, it can still be revealing of your desires, fears and inner demons.

Unfortunately, in order to write well and truthfully, and for your reader to identify with you, you have to open yourself up to some degree. This exposure is not always comfortable but most writers report that writing can be therapeutic, cathartic even.

Readers are generally simply happy to find that the characters in your work are believable. They will not delve too deeply into how much is based on the author's own feelings and experiences and how much is fictional or an amalgam of many real people.

Without doubt, it is always better to write from the heart and in truth. If you try to withhold certain aspects of your true self from your writing, it will dilute its effectiveness. Remember, as a last resort, if you are successful and are asked about the basis for a character, you can always be economical with the truth.

Writers' top tip 4: Age is no barrier

Never put off following your writing dream because you are not in the first flush of youth. There are plenty of successful writers who come to the profession later in life – some say that a lifetime of experience is a writer's greatest gift. The UK writer Penelope Fitzgerald launched her literary career at the age of 58 and won the Booker Prize for *Offshore* four years later. So what's stopping you?

Conscious procrastination

Now that we have relegated any subconscious fears that might have been preventing you from starting to write to their rightful place, let's take a look at the more straightforward category of wanton delaying tactics.

The *Chambers Dictionary* definition of procrastination is: 'the act or habit of putting off [what should be done immediately]'. Wikipedia expands this by saying: 'In psychology, procrastination refers to the act of replacing high-priority actions with tasks of lower priority.'

Because writers often work from home, the scope for replacing high-priority writing with lower-priority tasks such as hanging the washing, tightening a washer on a tap, or tidying the sock drawer is enormous. There is always something that you can persuade yourself needs doing urgently rather than actually spend any meaningful time writing. Do you recognize yourself in this?

Of course, there will be those of you among us who are extremely self-disciplined and who devote what little spare time you have to your writing projects (and you should feel free to leap to the next chapter if you're one of those lucky souls). But the vast majority of you (and I include myself in this category) can while away many a happy hour on trivial tasks in a thinly veiled attempt to put off the writing task at hand.

If you still find yourself engrossed in useless tasks rather than starting, why not try the following tips for curing procrastination?

▶ Set small, achievable goals and promise yourself a reward such as a cup of tea or a biscuit each time a goal is met.

▶ Clear your work area of clutter so that you do not get distracted.

▶ Don't be overambitious – you are unlikely to be able to maintain eight hours a day of solid writing or reach a target of 5,000 words a day, so don't expect it of yourself.

▶ Set yourself a deadline.

▶ Keep a log of how many times you've planned to start writing, only to put it off. It's humbling.

▶ Turn off your mobile, put the answerphone on, and ignore emails and social media – this is your time to write.

▶ Get the family on board – tell them about your deadline. That way, they will support you and make space for you.

▶ If there really is no spare time in your day to write, try getting up half an hour earlier until it becomes a habit.

Overdoing the planning

Usually, I keep telling students about the importance of research and planning because so often I see manuscripts that are littered with clumsy phrases, such as 'As I mentioned earlier…' – all due to the lack of planning when it comes to structuring articles and book chapters. This still holds true of course, but, in the context of getting started on a writing project, I have seen many writers spend an inordinate amount of time on research and planning, and it is simply because they are afraid to start the actual job of writing.

One lovely guy attending one of my ten-day writing workshops was writing an historical novel based around actual events, using some real and some fictional characters. His research and planning were breathtaking. He knew every detail of the period, the locations and the characters. He had the plot decided down to the last detail and even had family trees and profiles of all his characters, both main and supporting. Each day I would ask whether he had started writing, and his reply was unerringly that he had to put the finishing touches to yet another piece of the planning before he could start. I am delighted to say that he finally wrote a brief section of a chapter during our time together, but clearly the research and planning were a comfort to him while the writing itself filled him with fear.

This is such an easy trap to fall into for the novice writer. Over-planning and over-researching become an unconscious way of putting off starting to write. So, once you have collected a good body of research material together and you have a clear idea of the plot outline and characters, then it's time to switch from research mode to writing mode and get started.

Try it now: Organize your research

When you go through your research material, sort it into themes and put each piece of research into a related pile, or folder if you're working on screen. (I'm a Luddite and like to print off papers and then physically bundle them together under themes, marking each piece of paper/printout with a red letter so that I can instantly recognize in which section of the article/chapter the information belongs.) You will probably have the odd item that does not fit comfortably under any of your allotted headings – you can decide whether they need to go in or be dropped at a later date. Meanwhile, make a list of your themes/headings and decide in which order they should be covered in your book or article. Once you've decided on a beginning, middle and end to your feature or chapter, you will find that you have everything that you want to include in each section neatly collected together and the running order makes sense, so that your writing moves seamlessly from one topic to the next, and the reader is carried fluidly with you.

Knowing where to start

Easier said than done, I hear you cry. And I know that if you sit down with a blank screen in front of you and type Chapter 1 and then pause, the thought of a whole book lying ahead of you is a hugely daunting prospect. But who said you had to start on page one?

When I am writing a book, I rarely start with the first chapter, as would seem logical. In fact, I start with a chapter that really appeals to me, or one of the shorter chapters. It's a good way to get into the book and to stimulate your writing flow. I then return to the all-important opening chapter at a later date.

It doesn't matter if you start at the beginning or somewhere else; the important thing is to get something down on paper. Don't worry if it is not immediately perfect or it's not shaping up exactly as you planned. Just write whatever comes into your head and get all your ideas down – you will have the opportunity to edit and polish your work at a later stage.

Once you have committed your thoughts to hard copy, you will be amazed at just how encouraged and uplifted you feel. It's a great relief to have started and to be off the writing blocks, so to speak. You will now find it so much easier to tackle subsequent chapters of the book and to pull the whole project together small step by small step.

So, rather than seeing the book as an insurmountable task, break the project into manageable pieces that are not so disheartening. A 3,000-word chapter is a more manageable proposition than an 80,000-word novel. Once you've achieved this first goal, you need look no further than the next challenge, the next chapter – and little by little, you will find that you are nibbling away at what appeared to be a mountain and the job gets done.

Writers' top tip 5: Don't put off that tough chapter until last

Although it is fine to start writing at whichever chapter takes your fancy, I would add one word of caution here: tempting though it may be to leave the toughest chapter of your book until the very last moment, it is much better to tackle it when you are in the full flow of the writing process and when all is going well.

Try it now: Free-writing

At the start of my writing workshops, I get students to put aside their laptops and to find a pen and paper. We then spend about ten minutes 'free-writing', without taking the pen away from the paper. It doesn't matter what you write – it could be nonsense, it could be a stream of consciousness, an 'I remember when...' exercise or even a list, but the important thing is to keep writing continuously without pause for reflection or analysis. This is an exercise to kick-start creativity. Thoughts and ideas flow much more readily after this exercise, and it is then fine to go back to the laptop and start writing in earnest. Give it a try – you may be surprised at what your subconscious throws up. You may even be able to use it in your writing project.

Focus points

❋ Even professional writers are guilty of putting off the start of a writing assignment, but you simply have to take the plunge.

❋ Sometimes the reason for not starting to write is based on a subconscious fear. Once you have identified what your fears are, it is easier to put them aside and get down to work.

❋ There are tricks of the trade that can help you overcome conscious procrastination and time-wasting.

❋ Don't be tempted to put all your energies into research and planning – start your project *now*.

❋ Set yourself the modest goal of writing a chapter and, when you have completed that challenge, move on to the next one. This is far less daunting than viewing the project as one massive, insuperable whole.

Next step

Now you're all fired up and ready to go, let's take a quick look in the next chapter at some of the common mistakes to avoid when pulling your manuscript together ready for submission.

3

Self-editing

In this chapter you will learn:

- ▶ *How to improve your style*
- ▶ *How to choose the appropriate language and tone*
- ▶ *How to structure chapters*
- ▶ *How to avoid spelling mistakes and grammatical howlers.*

It's not the purpose of this book to try to teach you how to write. First, it would take a whole series of titles to cover that nebulous subject (but if you are after writing tips and don't mind a shameless plug, check out another of my books in the Teach Yourself series, *Write Fantastic Non-fiction and Get Published*). Secondly, you're probably doing a pretty good job of it anyway by this stage.

What I would say, though, having seen countless manuscripts from hopeful writers, is that there are some common pitfalls and traps that inexperienced writers often fall into. And these mistakes, to varying degrees, turn up all the time. I reason that, if you are aware of these snares, you can keep them in the back of your mind when you are writing and with any luck avoid getting caught yourself.

However, don't worry if your manuscript is already close to completion – it's not too late. Keep these dangers in mind when you are rereading or editing, and they will become glaringly obvious in your work now that you've had them pointed out to you.

Naturally, though, if you know what to avoid from the outset and steer clear of the common pitfalls, it will save you a lot of time in the long run.

Length

If you are to optimize your chances of getting published, then you have to recognize what a potential publisher is looking for. The majority of works of fiction are between 70,000 and 200,000 words, and most commonly in the region of 120,000 words. A non-fiction book is usually somewhere between 50,000 and 60,000 words in length. So, if your manuscript is very wide of this mark, be it too long or too short, you are compromising your chances of acceptance.

It doesn't matter if you have written the most astonishing, poetic, prize-winning prose, if your novel tops the 350,000-word mark it represents too much editing effort for a publisher to take on board. They may not even read it because it will seem like such a daunting prospect. Similarly, even the best advice will not cut it with a publisher if your self-help book barely scrapes 20,000 words.

You are also looking for chapters that are all roughly the same length. Some can be a bit shorter and some a little longer, of course, but as a general rule of thumb you are looking for chapters in a non-fiction book that are each somewhere around the 3,000- to 4,000-word count. Chapters can be longer in a novel but obviously don't have to be.

Writers' top tip 6: Length matters

Keep in the back of your mind the average length of successful manuscripts and make sure you are not too wide of the mark with yours.

Language

Unless you are writing an academic textbook, the favoured style of writing for non-fiction books is to use an open, accessible, informal kind of language that puts the reader at ease and establishes a rapport between the author and the reader. Some novice writers take that to mean that they should write as they speak, and, as a result, their language can become overfamiliar and over-jocular. 'How strong is your ego, matey?' was a sentence that cropped up in one manuscript that I was asked to critique, and that was just the tip of the iceberg.

Although it is good to talk directly to your reader – addressing them as 'you' is helpful – try not to become 'chummy' or too casual in your choice of language. Some expressions and types of language should be reserved for spoken English only.

An extension of this conversational style is the use of swearing in text. Unless it is in a novel or script (where it may be acceptable because of the characterization), you should avoid using any kind of expletives within your manuscript. You may well think that is blindingly obvious, but I can assure you that I have had to point this out to a fair few would-be writers. What you learn only through experience is that profanity in the spoken language is a regular and often barely perceptible fact of life, but in the written word it is ten times more powerful and shocking. Even in fiction, it should only be used when you want to make an impact or to suggest something about a character.

Another trap to catch out the unwary is the use of jargon and specialist language. This can be hard to spot if you are writing on a specialist subject, as the language perhaps appears everyday and acceptable to you. However, to the lay reader, if a book is littered with technical terms and jargon without any helpful explanation, then it is a big turn-off at best, and bewildering at worst.

The same rules apply to using colloquialisms. Unless you are very sure of your target market, or that these regional or subcultural expressions are understood by a wider audience, I suggest you avoid them wherever possible.

When writing a novel, you may well set the drama in a remote or overseas setting. This is fine and I'm sure you will be able to bring these unfamiliar locations to life for the reader by your descriptive writing, but beware of trying to write your characters' dialogue in a local dialect. It is incredibly difficult to get the language right and it often falls flat. For most writers, even those with years of experience (with a few notable exceptions such as Irvine Welsh), it is enough to allow the reader to imagine the patois in their heads when reading your words.

Finally, do not be tempted to change the way you use language just because you are writing. We have all heard jokes at the expense of the policeman who, when giving evidence, says something along the lines of 'I was proceeding in an orderly fashion in a westerly direction along Oxford Street, when I happened upon the suspect who was behaving in an erratic and suspicious manner...' Extreme, admittedly, but lots of new writers use stilted and formal language because they feel they must impress. For the same reason, they may also use lots of complicated and unfamiliar adjectives and adverbs, often because they can't decide which one is most appropriate. It's so easily done but it really is an ambush to try to avoid – keep your language simple and it will work harder for you.

Writers' top tip 7: Keep it simple

Use a simple rather than an elaborate word and use one adjective or adverb rather than two. This is not 'dumbing down' – it's making your writing accessible to the reader and keeping your meaning clear.

Try it now: Read your work out loud

If you are not sure if a sentence or paragraph is working, try reading it out loud. If it's hard to say, difficult to understand or is overlong, rewrite it and read it out loud again until it sounds sensible.

Style

One of the most common mistakes I find in the work of inexperienced writers is the tendency to use overly complex sentences requiring an excess of sub-clauses. This leads the writer into the trap of becoming overzealous in the use of commas (see below). This is often a result of having so much to say that several ideas get crammed into one sentence. However, it is better to simplify whenever possible. If you can, keep sentence length and complexity of ideas to a minimum. Fortunately, it is an easy mistake to correct as you can usually divide up a long sentence or paragraph using punctuation or by splitting it into two.

For the reader, shorter sentences help to speed up the pace and, conversely, longer sentences slow things down. By the same token, short paragraphs help to divide up the text into readily digestible bite-sized chunks, making it easier to read and to comprehend.

You are aiming for an average sentence length of about 15 to 20 words. Obviously, none of this is written in stone and, if you want to add a long sentence or paragraph to the mix occasionally, as I am doing right now, then that is absolutely fine. However, in the main, it is best to err on the side of keeping sentences short.

Whether you choose to write in an informal style or prefer a more literary, third-person approach is entirely up to you, but, whichever you choose, you must stick to it. If you keep changing the voice of the narrator, it will confuse your reader. It's also worth bearing in mind that, even if you opt for the more formal tone, your writing should still engage the reader.

Writers' top tip 8: One idea at a time...

If you work on the principle of one idea in a sentence and one topic per paragraph, this naturally curtails any tendency towards long-winded writing.

Try it now: Ration those adjectives and adverbs

This writing exercise always produces a groan when I use it on courses but it rams home the point about our reliance on adjectives and adverbs like no other. Write a descriptive piece of about 400 to 500 words – or give yourself about 20 minutes to write it – and make sure you use no adjectives or adverbs. In a group, we read it back out loud and the others have to spot whether an adverb or adjective has slipped in. You can mark your own work and then, once you are sure all are eradicated, you can add one adjective or adverb of your choice to lend emphasis. It really focuses the mind when these descriptive words are rationed and makes you think hard about how liberally and profligately we use them under normal circumstances.

Spelling, grammar and punctuation

The simple truth is that if your manuscript is littered with too many spelling mistakes or grammatical mishaps, it will not be taken seriously. Often mistakes creep in because you read and reread it so many times that you become blind to the mistakes. In addition, it is easy to introduce mistakes at the editing stage when you cut and paste copy, for example, and don't double-check that the sentences still make sense.

Whatever the reason, any agent or publisher faced with a high number of errors will simply drop your manuscript on the slush pile. If you want your book to be accepted, you have to remove the mistakes before you submit. Naturally, the odd little blunder will slip through the net, but your manuscript must not be teeming with such errors.

The golden rule is to always check and double-check your manuscript before submission. If spelling and grammar are not your strong point, then get someone else to check it for you.

Alternatively, for grammatical guidance, I suggest you take a look at Lynn Truss's book *Eats, Shoots and Leaves* (Fourth Estate, 2009), R.W. Burchfield's *Fowler's Modern English Usage* (Oxford University Press, 2004), Martin Manser's *The Good Word Guide* (A & C Black, 2011) or Philip Gooden's *Who's Whose?* (A & C Black, 2007).

Actually, while we're on the subject of 'who's' and 'whose', while the odd mistake will be overlooked, there are certain cardinal errors that will grate tremendously with any reader, publisher or agent and probably prejudice your chances of acceptance. So make sure you are fastidious about getting it right when it comes to the correct use of, to take the most obvious examples, 'its' and 'it's', 'who's' and 'whose', and 'there', 'they're' and 'their'.

In my experience, the most common thing guaranteed to trip up the unwary writer is punctuation. Whether it is as a result of the laxer rules of texting, I'm not sure, but the simple rules of punctuation are an anathema to many, it seems. Some writers use semicolons and colons like confetti, while you are lucky to get a comma out of others. Do you fall into one camp or the other? If so, again, Lynn Truss et al. can help out here – the rules are actually quite straightforward and easy to learn. If you take the time to refresh your memory and apply these punctuation guidelines diligently, you won't go far wrong.

I have saved the most irritating pitfall of punctuation till last: it is the use of exclamation marks and other typographical devices to lend emphasis in your writing. I will just say that these are to be avoided at all costs. A bald statement, but it's true. Exclamation marks, italicized or bold type to lend emphasis, or smiley faces (yes, I've seen those in manuscripts) are a sign of lazy writing. A statement should be striking enough in its own right and shouldn't need an exclamation mark to underline the fact. Please keep these stylistic banana skins to a minimum or, better still, avoid them completely.

Remember this

There is a saying that is doing the rounds on Facebook at the moment. It seems apt here: 'Grammar – it's the difference between knowing your shit and knowing you're shit.'

Clichés

George Orwell's advice to writers is still valid today. He said, 'Never use a metaphor, simile or other figure of speech which you are used to seeing in print.' Overused clichés are counterproductive because readers are known to switch off when they come across these hackneyed expressions in a text. So 'cold as ice' and its ilk should be consigned to the waste bin. If you can't come up with an alternative that is original and exciting, then simply don't use a metaphor or simile.

The same holds true of using hackneyed descriptions in your writing. I know certain publishers who will automatically bin a manuscript if there's any mention of dust motes dancing in sunlight as it filters through a windowpane anywhere in the text.

A final note of warning regarding clichés: if you're going to make up something original, make sure it works. No one likes a mixed metaphor, even though they can be very funny. One of my favourites was 'created' by an American radio announcer who said, 'Wake up and smell the coffee on the wall.' I think his enthusiasm got the better of him. Make sure your imagery makes better sense.

Writers' top tip 9: Be prepared to prune and pare

Aim to be clear, concise and precise wherever possible. When you're editing, watch out for rambling passages of text or where you've used two words where one will do (often because you cannot decide which word to drop), and ruthlessly cut these superfluous passages and words out. Your writing will be much tauter and more effective as a result.

Dialogue

I devote a whole chapter to characterization and dialogue (Chapter 7), but this section on self-editing would not be complete without a brief look at these major areas.

The beauty of dialogue for the fiction writer is that it is active – that is, it shows the character in action, rather than telling the reader about the character. This opportunity for exposition (prose that gives the reader information about the background of the characters or a situation) is often grasped eagerly by novice writers, but it is very easy for the execution to let you down.

The first warning here is to make sure that you don't get so carried away with the idea of revealing your character through dialogue that you end up with characters giving information that they would never give in real life. One stunning example I once received was: 'George, who is my 17-year-old son and your half-brother, has missed his plane.'

The other trap to avoid is where you give your characters grammatically perfect, superbly witty speeches that go on for pages. Dialogue should sound natural, even if it does not reflect how we actually speak (you don't have to include the small talk, umms and ahhs, and incoherent sentences that we use in everyday conversation). Try to keep a character's dialogue to three or four sentences of uninterrupted speech at the most; that way, you will avoid lengthy monologues and worthy diatribes.

Bear in mind when writing dialogue that it should:

▶ move the story forward

▶ reveal more of the character

▶ stick to the point

▶ be interesting

▶ be reasonably brief

▶ make sense to the reader.

Ordering

Perhaps the most common faux pas for new writers that I see is that they do not pay enough attention to the way in which a chapter or book is going to unfold. While the material for the chapter or book is carefully researched, no thought or planning is given to the way the text moves from one subject to the next. It all gets put in with scant regard to order. This leads to clumsy linking sentences like 'as I mentioned earlier' or 'as we have already seen' or, my particular pet hate, 'getting back to the subject of —— '. All of these jolt the reader from the world that you have created for them and break their train of thought. It also results in the text seesawing backwards and forwards with no thread running through it.

By breaking down the chapter into various subtopics, you can arrange your information and discuss it all at the relevant point in the chapter. Deciding on the order in which subtopics will appear means that you can move seamlessly from one point to the next, carrying your reader with you.

By the same token, if you have planned the ordering for a chapter/book, you can get to the main thrust of each section more quickly. Without planning, it is easy to include so much preamble (often with repeated promises of the 'later in this chapter you will find ...' kind) that your reader's attention flags and they give up. Once you have set the scene, get to the point of the chapter or book without delay – give the reader what they are after.

I once helped an author who had a wonderful idea for a self-help book that involved a game. However, he was so busy in the early chapters explaining the premise for this game and how it worked that over 200 pages passed before the reader got to the practical element of the book. Basically, you need to reward your reader for their effort sooner rather than later. If the action doesn't take place until Chapter 4, then make Chapter 4 your first or second chapter. I liken this experience to Christmas Day, when you are reading out the rules of a new board game to the assembled players and then realize that they've lost interest and gone off to play with something else. Keep the preamble to a minimum and get to the point as quickly as is decently possible.

This holds true for novels, too, where it's easy to fall into the trap of giving so much back story to your characters that nothing happens in your book.

Try it now: Work out your structure

To order my thoughts before writing a chapter of a non-fiction book or an editorial feature, I lay out all of my research on the desk and I identify the various topics that make up the piece. I give each topic a letter and then I categorize all of the pieces of research with one of the letters (literally writing on the sheet with a felt-tip pen). Then I gather the papers together and decide in which order they should appear. That way, nothing gets left out, and each part of the writing follows on smoothly from one to the next. Give it a go.

Writers' top tip 10: Say it only once

Watch out for repetition of ideas. Most of us can spot when we've repeated phrases or words, and these are easily changed. But watch out, too, for the trap of repeating the same idea but in several different ways. It should need saying only once.

Trying to be too clever

Yes, it's true. Most of us like to be a smart Alec. And in the case of writing, most of us cannot resist the temptation of showing just how much research we've done (and just how sophisticated our vocabulary is). Sadly, if you shoehorn every last piece of research you have into your book, your writing will become self-conscious and pretentious. A reader can smell showing off and will not appreciate being lectured on the minutiae of a subject. Only include knowledge that helps to shape your characters or the plot, if it's fiction, or helps the reader's understanding if it's non-fiction. Edit out the rest.

Focusing

It is easy to get so caught up in your writing that you lose sight of who you are aiming your book at. Your book is not for you; it is for a reader who knows less about the subject or the characters than you do. So make sure you continually check that you are explaining yourself clearly to your audience and that you are not taking things for granted. Try to reread your work through the eyes of an imaginary reader – this will help you make sure that your writing is concise, focused and accessible.

Writers' top tip 11: Avoid sentimentality

When writing fiction, don't confuse sentiment with sentimentality. The former is moving and comes naturally; the latter is mawkish and contrived.

Focus points

* Make sure your manuscript fits within the publishing industry's usual boundaries when it comes to its length and tone.
* If your manuscript is littered with spelling, grammar and punctuation mistakes, it will automatically be consigned to the slush pile.
* Avoid clichés and writing dialogue in dialect or 'accents'.
* Give attention to the order of each chapter before you write it.
* Don't try to be too clever or to impress; rather, try to inform.
* Always keep your target reader in mind when you write.

Next step

Once you have edited your manuscript and reread it over and over, you need to make sure that its presentation and layout don't let it down. We'll find out in the next chapter how to make your manuscript look the part.

4

Presentation and format

In this chapter you will learn:

▶ *Ways to present your manuscript so that it's easy to read*

▶ *How to avoid some of the common presentation pitfalls*

▶ *What to include and what to omit.*

You have finished your book, you have edited it and reworked it so that it is the best that it can be under your guidance, and you're ready to send your manuscript to an editorial service or to prospective agents and publishers (see Chapter 11). But is your sample material in good enough shape to send? By that I mean: is the manuscript looking presentable, readily accessible and easy to read?

It may sound as if I am asking the blindingly obvious but you would be surprised at how many submissions I see that are woefully inadequate in this regard. I cannot stress enough the importance of making the right impression from the outset with your submission. Agents and publishers see literally hundreds of manuscripts in a month, and you have just one shot at making a good impression. Why would you blow it by presenting shoddy, difficult-to-decipher work in a package that is impossible to open? Why would you not take the time to research the industry standards in terms of layout, style and presentation?

The guidelines for submitting manuscripts are pretty straightforward, and we will cover them all in detail in this chapter so that you give yourself the best chance of getting your work read and taken seriously from the outset. Even if you decide to stick to your own style, that is fine – none of this advice is written in stone and a great manuscript is not going to be turned down just because it has a few errors in it or it looks a little funky. However, make sure you apply some common sense – namely, that the style is consistent, that you are able to read the material easily and that it is not littered with mistakes.

Let's now turn our attention to the standard presentation for a submission.

Writers' top tip 12: No photographs

Don't include a photograph of yourself or your family with your submission. It will cut no ice, even if you are drop-dead gorgeous or your kids are cuter than cute can be.

Presentation

Although it is admittedly rare, occasionally handwritten manuscripts still drop on to publishers' and agents' desks and, sad to say, just as quickly they are usually dropped into the waste bin. In this technological day and age, I am afraid you are expected to type and print your manuscript before sending it off, as a bare minimum – publishers will not think it quaint that you have lovingly handwritten your book with quill and ink, so save yourself the effort.

Here's the received wisdom on how to present your typed work:

▶ **Line-spacing** Your manuscript should be double-spaced throughout (1.5 line-spacing is acceptable – actually that's what I use because it saves on paper when printing and this appeals to my green conscience / frugal nature).

▶ **Page numbering** Each page should be numbered sequentially throughout the book. Is there any other way to use page numbers? you may well be asking yourself. Well, actually, more than once I have received a manuscript in which the author starts each new chapter at page one. It doesn't sound like a heinous crime, I agree, but if page 13 flutters out of the pile to the floor, you have no easy way of knowing from which chapter it has fallen. And if you drop the lot, you have no chance.

▶ **Typeface** There is a big debate about which typeface to use but the truth is that most publishers and agents really do not care, just as long as the manuscript is legible. If your computer's default typeface is Times New Roman, then stick with it. If you prefer a more modern look, Georgia and Courier are the usual candidates. Choose a serif-based font – that is, one with decorative 'feet' attached to the strokes of the letters – as these are easier on the eye if you are reading for any length of time.

▶ **Font size** The ideal font size is 12 point, although this does slightly depend on the typeface you've chosen. Basically, too small is hard to read and too big makes your manuscript look juvenile.

▶ **Headers and footers** These are optional and I must confess that I don't usually bother. If you are a techno-whizz and you can easily put your name and/or title in dark grey as a header and/or footer, then feel free, but it's certainly not a prerequisite.

▶ **Chapters** Start each new chapter on a new page, number each chapter and give it a heading, and that is about all it takes, really. For simplicity, I type the chapter number and, on the line below, the heading at the start of the page and I put them both in bold, centred. Then, a couple of lines lower down, I start the body copy. You really do not need anything more elaborate than that. If you are using a quotation at the start of each chapter, which seems in vogue at the moment, this too should be centred and probably italicized.

▶ **Paragraph format** There is no need to insert a blank line between paragraphs. Instead, it is usual to indent the first line of every paragraph unless it follows a heading, in which case you keep it full out (against the left margin). A respectable and acceptable indent is the depth of one tab (by far the easiest way to achieve an indented paragraph, actually), but there is no right or wrong here as long as you are consistent.

▶ **Headings and subheadings** In non-fiction writing, headings and subheadings help to signpost the reader through your manuscript. The text can be much easier to understand if it is broken down into constituent parts using headings, and yet writers often use them sporadically and with no consistent style. Keep in mind that how you present your headings and subheadings conveys their importance. So subheadings should be consistently smaller than headings and any preceding subheadings. There is no firm rule for presentation, as long as you follow a tiered system and apply it consistently. The only other thing to bear in mind is that headings tend to be short and punchy, while subheadings can be longer and more explanatory.

▶ **Dates** The accepted format (in British English) for dates is: 18th December 1790 or 18 December 1790 – there is no need for 'the' and 'of,' as in 'the 18th of December'. I once edited a historical manuscript where every date was spelled out in words – 'the eighteenth of December'. Can you imagine how frustrating that became by the end of 80,000 words?

▶ **Numbers** A common style in publishing is that numbers from one to ten are written in words and 11 and above are written in numerals. However, in fiction a style of spelled-out numbers across the board is also common.

▶ **Acronyms** If you are writing on a specialist subject, there's every chance that you will be using acronyms. The industry standard is to write out the name in full on its first appearance in the text with the acronym in parentheses next to it - for example, the Royal College of Music (RCM) or repetitive strain injury (RSI). And thereafter you can just use the acronym.

There are some exceptions to this rule. For example, if you use the full name followed by the acronym in an early chapter but don't use it frequently, by the time you get to a much later stage of your text where you want to use it again, the lay reader has probably forgotten what it means. So, in this case, I would be tempted to write it out in full again. Another common solution where there are a lot of abbreviations is to provide a list at the beginning of the book.

▶ **Illustrations and diagrams** If you are writing a non-fiction book or a children's book, you may intend to include illustrations or diagrams in the published version. If you already have some to hand – say you are writing a local history and you have a collection of sepia, black-and-white and colour photographs, you could include a small selection with your manuscript – but it is not worth paying for the services of a professional illustrator or photographer at this stage. Nor should you be tempted to scan a few of your own sketches into the document, unless you are a very good, I'd even say professional, artist.

It is enough to type 'Diagram' in square brackets in the text to give a feel for how a finished book might look. If you are successful in your submission and you get a publishing deal, then you can discuss accompanying visuals at that point.

▶ **Printing** Despite the implications for paper wastage, you should print your manuscript on single-sided sheets as it makes the job of reading your book so much easier for a prospective publisher/agent – and let's face it, you don't want to irk them unnecessarily.

▶ **Spelling and grammar** We talked about this at length in the previous chapter, so I will simply reiterate here that you must take care with your spelling, punctuation and grammar. The odd mistake can and almost certainly will creep in, and that is acceptable. However, if your manuscript is littered with silly errors, especially in the first few pages, then it suggests that you will have shown a similar inattention to detail and lack of care in your writing.

▶ **Title page** Your manuscript should be faced with a title page on which you should include the title, your name and your contact details (address, phone number and email address). It doesn't have to be fancy – some authors really go to town with full colour illustrations and so on, but this is not necessary. The title should be in a large font size in the middle of the page, with your name in a slightly smaller font size a few lines below, and your contact information bottom left or bottom right, together with the word count in the opposite corner (this is optional but helpful, I find).

Writers' top tip 13: Don't bind the pages

Although it may seem unpolished to send off your manuscript without any binding, that really is the best option. Keep it loose-leafed with a large elastic band to secure it and that is it. Novice writers go to enormous lengths to comb-bind, staple and clip their manuscripts – I have even seen them where each chapter has been beautifully tied up with ribbon – but it is all unnecessary. Loose-leaf is the order of the day.

Writers' top tip 14: A fresh pair of eyes

If spelling and grammar are not your strong points, get someone else to read your manuscript looking for and correcting mistakes before you submit it. In fact, another pair of eyes can be useful even if you are quite proficient in this area.

Writers' top tip 15: Contact information is crucial

Don't forget to include contact information on the front page of your manuscript as well as in your covering letter, just in case the two become separated. You can also put it at the end as well if you want to be even more sure that it will be seen.

Try it now: Apply the guidelines

If you have a reasonable chunk of your manuscript already completed, go back to the first couple of chapters and re-edit them, applying the layout rules outlined in this chapter. Then put the manuscript aside for a few days. Finally, reread the edited chapters and a couple of the unedited chapters – it should then become apparent why these guidelines have come about over the years. The edited chapters should be easier to read.

Formatting dialogue

I have devoted an entire section to spoken words in text because it is the area of presentation where I see the most mistakes. Somehow, setting out direct speech sends writers into a panic. And yet the rules that govern its presentation are actually very straightforward. Once you have grasped them, apply them diligently and consistently and you will have no further problems.

The industry standard for setting out dialogue (at least in the UK; US style is a little different) is as follows:

▷ Use single or double quotation marks (Americans favour double; in the UK, we prefer single) at the beginning and end of a piece of direct speech.

▷ If dialogue runs over more than one paragraph, then you do not use closed speech marks at the end of a paragraph but you do use open speech marks at the beginning of each paragraph of the speech/dialogue. Only when you are at the end of the speech do you use closed speech marks.

▷ Each piece of dialogue (and/or each different speaker) starts a new, indented paragraph.

- Any action paragraph also starts a new, indented paragraph.

- There is no need for a capital 'S' for 'she said' when the preceding dialogue ends with a comma, question mark or exclamation mark.

- You use a comma rather than a full stop at the end of a bit of dialogue if you are continuing with a 'he said', 'she said' or an equivalent. In any other instance, you end a dialogue with a full stop inside the speech marks.

- Punctuation such as exclamation marks and question marks is kept within the speech marks. The same almost always applies to commas unless the sentence of dialogue continues beyond the 'he said' / 'she said'. For example: 'I have often wondered why', she said sadly, 'you came back.'

- If you have used single speech marks for your dialogue, then you should use double speech marks for any quoted speech within the dialogue. For example: 'He was always telling me "You're so stupid" but I never listened!'

Another rule that often causes consternation for new writers is whether or not to ascribe the dialogue to a named character. In fact, when writing dialogue between two people, there is no need to insert 'he said' or 'she said' after every line of dialogue. The reader can work out that we take it in turns to speak, so only add the occasional 'he said' if you think the reader might be losing track of whose turn it is.

It might be helpful if I give an illustration of a conversation laid out in the conventional way to make all these rules clearer:

'Why aren't you at work?' asked Sheila.

'The foreman sent me home,' Tony said, avoiding Sheila's eyes and busying himself with the padlock on the table.

'Did you do something wrong?'

'Not me. I just got caught in the crossfire.'

'Let me guess which one of your deadbeat mates has got you into trouble now. I'll bet Peter was involved.'

If you ascribe an action to one of the speakers during the dialogue, you might then want to identify the speaker who resumes the conversation, so that it is perfectly clear to the reader. Otherwise, you can simply carry on the alternating pattern of conversation without the addition of 'he said' or 'she said'.

Writers' top tip 16: Keep to 'he/she said'

One of the most common mistakes made by novice writers is that they feel the need to come up with alternatives to 'he said' and 'she said'. The dialogue then becomes laden with clumsy words such as 'exclaimed', 'retorted', 'protested', 'demanded', 'opined', 'cried out', 'rejoined', 'interjected' and even 'expostulated'. And so the awkward and archaic list goes on. Experienced writers tend to stick with a simple 'said' – you would do well to take a leaf out of their book.

Try it now: Transcribe a dialogue

The only way to make sure you have fully grasped the rules for dialogue is to practise it for yourself. So, using your smartphone or a digital voice recorder, record a brief snippet of conversation from the television, or a chat that may be going on in your home. (If you tell someone what you're doing, they will become self-conscious and their speech will become unnatural and strained; on the other hand, if you don't tell them and you pick up something unflattering to the speaker, it could lead to a domestic tiff. I leave this judgement call to you.) Transcribe the conversation, inserting the occasional 'he said' and 'she said' to make it more realistic. Then read it back, checking it against the dialogue format rules outlined above. If you practise a few times, it soon becomes second nature.

Remember this: Postage and packaging

When you're ready to package up your manuscript and proposal, avoid securing it so tightly that the recipient cannot get into it. There is nothing more frustrating than a package that is impossible to open. And please make sure you put the right postage on the package. This might sound like a no-brainer but publishers still receive packages with excess postage to pay – sure enough, these manuscripts rarely get read.

Focus points

* Presentation is important but, ultimately, it is not as crucial as getting your writing right, so don't worry too much about it.
* There are accepted norms for layout but as long as it is clearly spaced and legible that should be enough.
* Don't sabotage your chances before your manuscript is even read by making the packaging almost impossible to open or not paying enough postage.
* Always keep a hard and/or electronic copy of your manuscript.

Next step

All books, irrespective of genre, are there to perform a function, be it to entertain, to inform, to inspire, or all three. In the next chapter we will take a look at how it is often easy to forget the purpose of why you are writing.

5

Fit for function?

In this chapter you will learn:

▶ *How to identify the key components of certain genres*

▶ *How to make sure your manuscript lives up to its billing*

▶ *How to recognize the marketing classifications used by publishers*

▶ *The purpose of particular features often found in a book.*

This chapter is devoted to an aspect of publishing to which most writers do not give due consideration. In fairness, when you are experiencing the first flush of excitement at the beginning of your writing project, it is hardly surprising that you are not giving too much thought to exactly where your book might one day sit in a bookshop or library or in which Amazon category. Nonetheless, if you know what genre of book you are writing and you always keep that in the back of your mind, you will be surprised at just how much it helps you to keep your writing on track and how much it improves your book's marketability.

Not sure what I'm talking about? Well, what if I told you that I have read self-help manuscripts with no discernible practical advice given, travel guides devoid of any description and character-driven novels where none of the characters develops throughout the book? In all these cases, the writer has lost sight of the purpose of the genre and the book is not fit for function and, as a result, pretty much unviable.

So, it is important throughout the writing process to occasionally ask yourself if your book will give your reader what they want. Is it doing what it is supposed to do? Does it fulfil the purpose/ brief for the style of book you have decided to write?

As a creative, you may not like the idea of being constrained by any parameters, and I can understand and sympathize with that. However, the publishing industry is a business that is segmented by genre, and in order to write relevant, publishable books, you need to know which genre you are targeting and you need to follow trends within your genre. For example, fantasy has been a genre that has been growing in popularity in recent years. So it was exciting news for fiction writers when, recently, a new genre appeared on the bookshelves, namely Dark Fantasy. A fine distinction between the two, you might be thinking, but this is music to the ears of the fantasy writer, because it means that book sellers will now be looking to buy Dark Fantasy to stock those empty shelves; *ipso facto*, publishers will be wanting to publish Dark Fantasy books and agents with their fingers on the pulse will be seeking to represent writers of Dark Fantasy.

Keeping your book in genre

It doesn't matter which particular genre of book you are writing, the same principle holds true. When a publisher is considering your manuscript, she will be wondering in her mind's eye where this book will be positioned by the booksellers as well as how it will sit alongside other books on their list. Whether or not it complements other commissions is out of your control, but how your book is categorized is something you can think about.

A crucial element in the lengthy process of getting a raw manuscript to publication is played by the sales team who are going to try to sell your book into the bookshops – and, for that to be successful, they have to know how to categorize it and to be able to tell a bookseller on which shelf it will sit. If the sales team do not give your synopsis their backing at the editorial meeting, it is unlikely to progress any further, despite the support of an enthusiastic editor. So ask yourself: does my novel belong to the historical fiction or romantic fiction category? Does my personal-development non-fiction title sit under Religion and Spirituality or is it a self-help guide? Then, once you've decided which genre it sits within, you can ask yourself whether your manuscript is fulfilling the purpose of this type of book.

Here are a few pointers to help you to identify your genre and to help to steer your book so that it remains relevant and publishable.

Writers' top tip 17: Keep on trend

It doesn't matter which of the book genres you are writing in; make sure you stay aware of changes and trends within the genre as this can make a difference to the viability of your book in a publisher's eyes.

SELF-HELP OR HOW-TO BOOKS

The readers of this genre of book are generally looking to increase their specialist knowledge, bolster personal, social or professional skills, and/or resolve personal issues. Basically, if you are writing a book in this genre, you have to make sure that you meet at least one of these three requirements.

Essentially, you have to share some specialist knowledge with your reader. You may be writing a self-help book that is based on your own personal experiences, so there will be a lot of memoir in your manuscript, and this can work fine, too, as long as you remember that this genre is expected to offer practical advice. It is up to you to make sure you get the balance right.

Remember this: Aim for the right length

Most non-fiction self-help books are in the region of 50,000–60,000 words in length. I often receive manuscripts that fall short of this target by quite some way, and this automatically puts an obstacle in the path of finding a publisher for these books.

Sometimes this genre takes the form of either a step-by-step or modular book. You can use these styles if you have a specific programme for solving a problem that perhaps involves progressively learning new skills; if you want to explain to the reader how they can develop skills by following an evolutionary process of steps; or when the content of your book can be broken down into clear component parts, which together give the reader a new skill or solve a problem.

The writing style of self-help and how-to books has to be easy and accessible – you want just the right tonal mix of the reassuring and sympathetic, yet authoritative. I see a lot of manuscripts that are written by experts with much valuable knowledge to share, but the tone is didactic and removed, and sometimes patronizing. This is not a good way to get your reader on side.

And you do have to have something to offer to write self-help books. Non-fiction publishers usually favour an author who has some experiential or professional credentials to offer, so if you were writing a self-help book about attaining happiness, for example, they would probably expect the author to be a practising psychologist, counsellor, life coach, therapist, etc., or to have a good reputation as a speaker/workshop leader in this field. If the book is purely based on your own life experiences, then I'm afraid that is probably not enough to get you a publishing deal.

By the same token, even writers who appear to have the right credentials to pen a self-help book fall into the trap of simply proffering their opinions without being able to substantiate these in any detail. Statistics, facts and case studies can go some way to supporting your views – in fact, bold or startling facts and figures about a topic are great for capturing a reader's attention and introducing drama into a subject that may not be that exciting – but the fact remains, if you are flying in the face of proven, received wisdom based on your own experience alone, it will not be enough to persuade a publisher.

Remember this: Have the right credentials

You must have some relevant credentials that qualify you to write a self-help or how-to book, whether they are experiential or professional qualifications. And it helps if you are still practising in the field in some way, so that the publisher knows that your knowledge is current, and preferably cutting-edge.

If you get the balance right between expert advice, inclusive tone and reader participation, and you tailor your book to your target audience, then you are making it easier for a publisher to see how the end product might be marketable.

Try it now: Test-pilot your self-help book

Hobbyist self-help books sometimes include step-by-step instructions to help a reader to make something. I wrote a series of survival books for adolescent boys (under the pen name Rory Storm), which included directions for starting fires, making pot-holders, digging snow holes and so on. To make sure the instructions made sense to a novice reader, I would inveigle my unsuspecting sons into following the directions unsupervised by me, to see if they could produce results using the instructions alone.

Why not write a set of instructions for a task and then find a volunteer to follow them? Make sure you include what they will need and how much time it will take as well as the step-by-step actions. Your volunteer will be able to tell you whether your instructions are clear and easy to follow or whether they are ambiguous or lacking in essential details.

Writers' top tip 18: Triumph over adversity

A personal memoir that is a 'triumph over adversity' story can be popular with publishers but, for it to be successful, it has to have an overall upbeat and inspiring message and not leave the reader feeling more depressed than when they started. The clue is in the title – keep 'triumph over adversity' in the back of your mind and avoid the 'adversity heaped upon more adversity' storyline.

TRAVEL BOOKS

If you have set yourself the challenge of writing a travel book, then there are certain prerequisites that a publisher would expect in your manuscript, however quirky or off-the-wall your idea. It may seem self-evident to say that description is an essential part of travel writing, but some novice writers believe an account of the location that's full of hyperbole and superlative adjectives is enough. In fact, the aim of travel writing is to give your reader a real sense of a destination, by appealing to all five senses. As well as evoking the spirit of the place, however, you must also give practical, useful information, in case your reader is inspired to pay a visit.

Most destinations have been written about before on numerous occasions. In order to pique a potential publisher's curiosity, you need to find a new and original approach to the location and write it from that angle. One of the most successful travel books to demonstrate this principle is Tony Hawks's *Round Ireland with a Fridge* (Ebury Press, 1999), which went on to spawn a television documentary. This has set a trend that is hard to ignore, from destination guides such as *Travels with Tinkerbelle: 6,000 miles around France in a Mechanical Wreck* to travel books on things to do (*747 Things to do on a Plane*) and themed books (*Recession-busting Britain*).

Writers' top tip 19: Find a new angle

Try to find a new and original approach to a location and write your travel guide from that angle.

Try it now: Write a short travel piece

Write a short description of a place or an event that has made an impact on you. It doesn't have to be a holiday destination – it could be a stately home you've visited, a mountain view or a spiritual festival. Use language that evokes the sights, sounds, smells and feel of the occasion and add details that you remember. Keep it brief – about 500 to 750 words – but remember to include the vital ingredients of good travel writing – sensual descriptive appeal, personal input, detail and information.

CHILDREN'S BOOKS

The most common mistake made by novice writers of children's books is that they underestimate how hard it is to write for children and they underestimate their audience. Don't ask me why, but a myth has grown up that writing fiction and non-fiction for kids is somehow easier than writing for adults. If anything, the converse is true, because a young audience is a lot less forgiving and much more fickle than a grown-up readership.

The second biggest misconception surrounding children's fiction is that, just because your own children enjoy your made-up bedtime stories, your creations will automatically become a bestselling children's book. Sad to say, your children are a captive audience who love having your time and attention at bedtime – they are not impartial judges of your writing ability.

Remember this: Don't patronize your readers!

If children get the slightest notion that you are talking down to them, they will abandon your book without hesitation. Do not patronize your young audience, whatever you do.

It is also important to tailor your book to a specific age group. Just as publishers are looking to fit adult books into a certain genre, the same is true for children's books, with the added dimension of recognized age bands. Once you know these ages (see box), then it is easier to write using an age-appropriate language and style rather than using a loose, scatter-gun approach in the hope of attracting as many readers as possible.

Children's books: age bands

* **Picture books** are appropriate for pre-readers aged up to five years old, although some children's non-fiction publishers are happy to take picture books (where the illustrations play as important a role as the text in telling the story) for an older age range, say up to eight years old.

* **Early reader books** (aka easy readers) are for children aged five to eight who are just starting to read on their own. They are often specifically designed to help a child expand his or her vocabulary and reading skills.

* **Chapter books**, for children aged seven to ten, have short chapters and still have relatively short paragraphs for the younger readers. However, longer chapter books are available for nine- to twelve-year-olds. These books tackle more sophisticated themes and cover topics such as biography, science, history and multicultural themes.

* **Young adult**, which are predominantly for twelve-year-olds and upwards, often cover topics that are pertinent to today's 'tweenies' and teenagers. They are aimed at children who have outgrown the chapter books but are not yet ready for subjects that 15-plus-year-olds might read.

If you are going to write for children, for heaven's sake take it seriously. Why do authors take a professional approach to writing for adults, yet believe they can dash off a book for kids in their spare time? You must approach the research and writing of characters and plot for a children's book in exactly the same way as you would for an adult audience. The only difference in the writing process is the style and type of language that you use. Everything else is the same.

A popular genre for children's books at the moment is narrative non-fiction, also known as creative non-fiction. This is where actual events and characters are brought to life by weaving a fictional story around them. Could this be a way for you to enliven the knowledge you want to share?

And, finally, it's worth bearing in mind that you are playing to a tough audience – one with a low boredom threshold and which is used to the instant gratification of computers and television. You must grab your readers' attention from the outset.

Try it now: Write a short piece of children's fiction or non-fiction

The language you use when writing for children has to be interesting and vivid, yet readily understandable. You often have to translate complex ideas and information into words that children can understand. Why not have a go at writing a short passage aimed at a certain age category of children's books? It could be a short story or an explanation of a historical or scientific event – you choose – but make sure you bring your subject to life before the eyes of your young readers.

Here are a few style tips that might help:

* Have fun with language. You can spice up your text by using onomatopoeia, alliteration, homonyms, double entendres, humour and rhyme.

* Use examples from the child's world to help them understand complex ideas or information.

* Use similes, metaphors and comparisons. For example, try comparing sizes to something familiar so that the child has a point of reference: 'A giant squid's eye has the largest eyes of any animal – at 39 cm across, it is 16 times wider than a human eye.' Just make sure your points of reference are relevant to today's children – most will not know what an LP is, for instance.

* Build a conspiratorial bond with your reader by being friendly and talking directly to the individual. Involve him or her by using an informal conversational style – 'Bet you didn't see that coming!'

* Ask questions.

* Vary your sentence length.

If you're writing non-fiction, stick to the facts, but there is nothing to stop you bringing the child into your world by using the second person – 'Imagine a fire broke out in your school. You would have to keep cool and act fast.'

If you're writing fiction, you can be as outrageous and imaginative as you like. It won't seem extreme to children, who have the most vivid imaginations of all.

Writers' top tip 20: Keep a narrow focus

Children are interested in details. So, although it sounds counter-intuitive, don't be afraid to narrow down your subject. Think of *War Horse* (Egmont, 2006), the bestselling book written by Michael Morpurgo. He could easily have written a story about the First World War from a human viewpoint, but chose instead to focus on the role of horses in that conflict.

FICTION

What do you expect to get from reading a novel? A gripping plot? Believable and beguiling characters? Heroes and villains? Witty dialogue? Do you hope to learn about other lands or epochs?

We each have favourite genres of fiction but most of us expect much of the above list as basic requirements of a good read. The difficulty for a fiction writer is that, if you focus on one aspect of the writer's craft, say characterization, it can be to the detriment of another aspect such as plot development.

It is natural to play to your strengths. So, if you happen to be gifted with the ability to write pithy dialogue, it's a fair bet that that you will use it liberally in your narrative. However, it is essential that you do not neglect the other aspects of fiction writing altogether or your novel will not deliver what it promises or what it should.

The other trap for the unwary author of novels is that it is tempting, after spending so long on the research for your book, to show just how clever you are and how much you know. This, again, will be to the detriment of your writing. A reader/publisher can spot instantly when material is included simply to impress rather than for the benefit of the storyline. You don't have to include every piece of research – select what is pertinent and leave the rest. Your research has done its job in informing your understanding of the background to your story, and you will write a better novel because of it.

The purpose of elements of books

Quite often I will receive a manuscript that has all the component parts you would expect from a non-fiction book (for example an introduction, glossary and conclusion) but these parts fail to fulfil their intended purpose. Here, we'll take a look at some of the constituents of a book and why they have evolved, and in that way you can make sure you get these parts of your manuscript right if and when you include them in your book.

INTRODUCTIONS

An introduction is a gift for a writer as it is the first opportunity to talk to your reader directly and to form a rapport with them. You can give them any background information that you think might prove useful – for instance, why you wrote the book or what they might expect to get from reading it. You are also at liberty to be more personal than you might be in the main body of the manuscript – perhaps describing your hopes and aspirations for your book.

The function of an introduction is to get your reader comfortable with you and to whet their appetite for what is to come. It helps them to slip into the book as if into a hot bath, warming them gradually. It is not just another chapter of the book. The style can be different and the tone more informal or intimate. While they are a gift to a writer they are also a double-edged sword because, although it is a perfect opportunity to establish a relationship with your reader, quite a few people do not actually read an introduction in their eagerness to get started. So, just in case, don't include anything in the introduction that is crucial to the main body of the book.

And bearing in mind that most readers are chomping at the bit to get going, keep your introduction relatively brief – 750 to 1,500 words is about right.

SOURCES

Writers who make the transition from academic and scientific books to mass-market books often include sources within the body of the text. If you are writing a popular book, this is not required. You simply have to keep your references available for the publisher in the event that there is a query after publication.

CONCLUSION OR CONCLUDING CHAPTER

Your final chapter is an opportunity to tie together all the loose ends and themes that you have threaded through the book. While you do not have to make the ending too neat, it does have to satisfy any curiosity that may still linger in the reader's mind.

I quite often see manuscripts where the writer has obviously been unsure how to conclude their project, and you get a strong sense that they have simply run out of steam. The concluding chapter dictates the final impression that your reader will be left with so, even if you're struggling to come up with a good ending, at least make sure it is decisive – that the reader knows you have purposely finished on a flourish rather than just petered out.

APPENDICES

These are not common, but they can serve a useful function in a non-fiction book. For example, you may have information that you want to include but which is not integral to the main point of your book and whose inclusion in the main body would slow down the pace too much. In that case, add it as an appendix. Those who are sufficiently interested will turn to those pages, and those who are not will continue to read without any interruption to their flow of thought.

GLOSSARY

A glossary is very useful in both specialized non-fiction books and in fiction set in a period or location that may be unfamiliar to most readers, or that uses unusual technical terms or jargon. If you keep inserting an explanation for words or phrases in parentheses in the body copy, it can be distracting and again it can slow the pace. It is better by far to use a glossary – though you should keep it brief. One inexperienced author sent me a manuscript in which the glossary was almost as long as the book and the explanations stretched to several pages. That is not what a glossary is for. It is simply to shed light on any terminology that you think might not be understood and whose meaning is essential to the reader's comprehension of the text or story.

Focus points

✻ Make sure you think about what a reader/publisher expects to get from your genre of book.

✻ Familiarize yourself with the genres and classifications of books used by publishers and booksellers.

✻ Make sure you have some credentials or experience that qualify you to write your book.

✻ Understand the constituent parts of your book and what their function is.

✻ Always keep the target reader in mind and tailor your language and approach accordingly.

Next step

You now know what you have to include in your book so that it fits happily within its genre. In the next chapter you will discover ways to make sure that your writing stays on track.

6

Staying focused

In this chapter you will learn:

▶ *How to keep your reader in mind*
▶ *Ways to make sure you stick to your plot*
▶ *How to recognize what is relevant and what's not*
▶ *How to get the right order in chapters and books*
▶ *Ways to keep going when things get tough.*

How many times have you started to read a book that shows great promise, only to put it down unfinished because it appears to go off the boil or you lose interest? Often, that is not because the author has suddenly ceased to be able to write engagingly: it is rather that they have 'lost the plot', so to speak. They have veered from the way you thought the writing was shaping up or got tangled in subplots, and, as a consequence, they have lost your attention.

Whether you are writing fiction or non-fiction, a screenplay or a script, keeping certain aims in mind will improve your work considerably. If you always remain aware of the person you are writing for (your audience) and what the book hopes to achieve (the aim), you are more likely to keep your writing tight and focused.

Throughout the writing process you should keep asking yourself whether the chapter or scene you have just written is on target for your readership/audience, whether it helps to fulfil the aims of your book/play and whether the information enhances the reader's/viewer's/listener's understanding. After that, when trying to keep your focus, there are a few fundamental differences that are unique to non-fiction and fiction.

Non-fiction writing

The key to staying focused in non-fiction writing is planning. The purpose of non-fiction in all its various guises is to impart knowledge or skills and to inform the reader. Given this aim, your first task is to plan what information you want to share, and, most importantly in the context of this chapter, you must then work out the logical progression of how you are going to share it and in what order.

We've already touched on ordering in Chapter 3, but it is fundamental to this chapter, too, so I'm going to expand on the theme.

By the very nature of non-fiction, you are helping the reader to expand their knowledge or their skillset. So you will probably have a lot of facts, tips and advice to impart. Whether your advice follows a programme so that the reader progressively learns new skills (as in step-by-step books) or is broken into component parts that together give the reader a new ability (modular books), you must categorize all your research and information into natural groups and then decide in which order these groups of information are presented. In that way, you have decided your chapter breakdown and order.

Remember this: It doesn't have to be chronological...

Even if your non-fiction book is a personal memoir or a family history, you don't necessarily have to write it as a chronology, which can be quite restricting. You may well prefer to think of themes and use these to order your chapters rather than follow a timeline.

Writers' top tip 21: Work out a structure

Invest time before you start writing in working out the themes and order of your chapters and the information within them, and this will help to keep you on track when you start writing.

Once you have decided on a beginning, middle and end to your chapter, you'll find that your writing moves seamlessly from one theme to the next, from paragraph to paragraph, and the reader is carried fluidly through the chapter, and the book. This avoids the common mistake that many writers make of seesawing backwards and forwards between subjects, veering off at tangents, only to return via a circuitous route to an earlier topic, often with the use of clumsy linking phrases such as the evergreen 'As I mentioned earlier...'

While we're on the subject of sifting through your research to work out how you are going to order your material, I'll mention another snare that catches out many an unwary writer – the temptation to include every last bit of research that you have found. The understandable reasoning behind this is that you do not want to waste the results of all your hard graft, but the logic of that argument is flawed. Tempting as it may be, it is a false move to include everything. If you try to pack it all in, it will lead you up blind alleys from which it is hard to extract yourself. The inclusion of too much unnecessary information slows the pace and takes you away from the main focus of each chapter.

Writers' top tip 22: Use your research wisely

Make sure you include only the most pertinent facts from the most credible sources that are essential to the understanding of the reader. Any more is superfluous – you will lose your reader's focus and it can also smack of 'showing off'.

Another temptation that you should resist at all costs is the desire to add your own opinions to your non-fiction writing. Whereas it is perfectly acceptable to offer advice based on personal experience if you have the relevant credentials to be writing an advice book, it is not advisable to litter your text with what are essentially your personal views, many of which are probably irrelevant. If you are a high-profile expert or a celebrity writer, then people might be interested in your views – for the rest of us, the reader really is not that fascinated by what you think privately, so keeping it to yourself is the best idea.

I have seen some submissions where the author's voice has overstepped the mark and become too opinionated. A manuscript for a slimming guide, for example, included such comments as 'In days gone by when food packaging did not include nutritional information, people were much slimmer' and 'You do not associate being overweight with being neurotic', which is dangerously close to the cliché that all fat people are jolly. Then there was the proposed book on dating where the male author included this piece of advice to single women: 'Just as women want their men to be tall, dark and handsome, the provider, the protector and the gentleman, so do men want their women to be beautiful, vulnerable, the bearers of our children and, last but not least, absolute ladies' – as well as the astonishingly outdated 'If he truly loves you, he will marry you.' Neither of these authors possessed any credentials that qualified them to write a book on their chosen specialist subject, and these were clearly their personal views based on their own particular life experiences. It might be a fascinating insight, but opinions and asides do not have a place in professional writing – they simply distract the reader and divert the text from staying on track.

Try it now: Plan a magazine feature

Planning a book is a gargantuan task, so let's scale it down and do an exercise that helps to show the importance of planning and ordering. Imagine you are going to write a 1,500-word magazine feature on the topic of your proposed book. Collect together all the material you would like to include. Now decide how you want to join all the component parts and in which order, so that the feature becomes a cohesive and coherent whole. You might like to make a linear plan, putting elements into their order of importance. Or you might prefer to group pieces of information into common themes (the method I use and describe in Chapter 3). Then write up your collected research in the order that you have preordained, and see if the feature stays on track and runs smoothly.

Remember this: Keep your reader in mind

The writing style and tone of your book have to stay on track, too. The best way for that to happen is for you to know your target reader and to keep that person in mind when you write, so that the style, language and tone are tailored exactly to your audience. If the readership is similar in age to you, then imagine you are coaching and supporting a friend, for example. Clearly, a book aimed at young freestyle snowboarders is going to use a different style and tone from one aimed at retired allotment gardeners.

Fiction writing

In some ways, it is even harder to stay focused and on track with fiction, as your imagination is limitless and anything could happen in your plot. You really can go off on flights of fancy as the mood takes you, but this tends to result in your reader being left to wonder why you have gone off on this particular tack, and the storyline often suffers.

When writing fiction, one of the best ways to keep the plot tight and focused is to keep questioning your motives. From the very beginning, when you're thinking about loose plot ideas, even if you only have an opening scene, a few major incidents and a possible ending in mind for your novel, write each plot development down. Now, start with your opening idea. Ask yourself 'Why this character and why this situation?' and come up with as many answers or follow-on questions as you like. It helps to form the back story for the character and to furnish you with the incidents in the story that have led up to where you start in your book (what sort of upbringing did your main character have? Loving? Brutal? Wacky?). The majority of this information is purely for you and it probably will not even feature in your novel, but it helps you to formulate the remaining plot based on a deep understanding of your character and what motivates him or her.

You can use this device with all the key plot developments that you come up with. The fact that there could be multiple answers to each question doesn't matter; write them all down (many authors use mind maps), explore the strengths and weaknesses of each possibility and then decide which one is the best for your storyline. Let's look at an example. A monk is going to abandon his vocation and there can be any number of reasons for his actions. Perhaps someone from his life before he took holy orders has reappeared and unsettled him; perhaps he has become disillusioned with the Church; possibly there has been an old friend who has been murdered and he feels that he has to return to the real world to solve the mystery and see justice done; or, rather more prosaically, perhaps he has a drink problem and the abbot has kicked him out. I'm sure you could come up with many more suggestions and only you will know which answer is the best to match the tone and the twists and turns of your plot.

Once you understand the back story to key points in the book, you can then ask yourself, 'Where does the story go from here?' So, to continue the above example, the monk could leave his order and solve the crime; he could rail against the Church and become a social activist; or he could fight his alcohol addiction and start a spiritual sanctuary for addicts.

The real point of these searching exercises is twofold. Firstly, if you keep asking yourself these questions as you develop the plot, it helps you to avoid going with the first idea that pops into your head, which is not always the strongest. And secondly, and most importantly for this chapter, it keeps the plot on track and running seamlessly, without diversions that haven't really been thoroughly thought through.

Writers' top tip 23: Don't make up the story as you go along

If you know the back story to characters and events, it helps you to avoid unbelievable motivations and problematic plotting. Avoid trying to make up the story as you go along unless you have a good deal of experience of writing fiction.

Try it now: Come up with a plot

Most plots develop because a character is in a situation involving conflict. The conflict might be a personal dilemma, an ambition, a threatening enemy, an onerous duty, or the loss of something important. In most stories, a series of choices leads, ultimately, to the problem being resolved. Often, the resolution arrives because the external situation is different (the ambition is achieved, the enemy vanquished, and so on). Just as often, and especially in contemporary stories, something changes internally in the character after the story's resolution. He or she gains an insight, adopts a new philosophy, or comes to terms with a negative emotion. Have a go at this plotting exercise.

Think of a basic plot outline using the following character and situation: a 30-year-old writer is about to have her first book published. She encounters an old colleague who knows a secret about her. Based on this situation, what would happen first? What next? Think about what kind of climax or resolution might occur in this plot. Can you come up with a basic plot outline?

There is one last question that you should always ask yourself, not only at the beginning of your writing project but throughout the process, and that is: What do I want my reader to experience and feel when they read my book? And do you want the emotions you are trying to engender to change as the reader moves through the story? Perhaps you want the reader to be wary of a supporting character initially but to grow to like and respect him as his unfolding actions and behaviour earn the reader's trust. Could it be that you want to provoke anger in your reader about a situation or sympathy for a cause?

This is not something you need to ask yourself constantly, but keeping in mind the effect you want your book to have on your reader helps you avoid creating any plot twists and turns or character developments that are out of harmony with your aim.

In my job as a journalist, I have had to interview countless authors and it always surprises me when they are ill prepared for these seemingly harmless questions – namely, 'What are your ambitions for this book?' and 'Why this topic?'

In fact, it can be useful to think about the answers to these standard interviewers' questions while you are writing your book because, once again, it helps you to keep focused and to stay on track. So indulge me a moment and picture this scenario. Imagine your book has just been published to great critical acclaim. You are being interviewed for a TV or radio book or arts show. The interviewer asks you the question, 'What did you hope to achieve with your book?' followed by 'Why this theme for your first book?' What do you reply?

If you know the answer to these questions while you are writing, you will make sure that your plot and your characterization all combine to achieve your ambitions for the book. Whether it's to create a work of high literature, to draw attention to the plight of a minority group or to make working mothers with pre-school kids laugh at the absurdity of trying to raise a family while sitting in the boardroom, whatever the ambition, keep it in mind and you will not stray far from the right path.

Remember this: Use subplots sparingly

Many writers use subplots as a way to divert the reader from the main action and to raise the suspense. Subplots usually involve minor characters in your book and contrast with the central narrative. However, don't be tempted to include too many subplots as these can overwhelm the action and distract the reader from the central plot.

Writers' top tip 24: Research should play second fiddle

Resist the temptation to show your reader just how much you know about the subject within your novel – it can get boring. Keep your eye on the theme of your book and only include specialist research if it benefits the plot or characterization.

Staying the course

Writers who experience problems staying on track often never finish a project or their ventures morph into something else. Does this ring any bells?

Basically, we all love the excitement of starting a project – coming up with the initial idea, shaping it and making it into something exciting and promising. Many of us also love the process of starting to write – getting your teeth stuck into the project, if you like. But it is also fair to say that many struggle once the project has been under way for a while. The initial euphoria has worn off and it is becoming a hard slog. You start to find reasons to avoid going to your computer to write.

It is generally at this point that, being the creative person that you are, you come up with another new and shiny idea – perhaps an even better idea, you persuade yourself. Then it becomes all too easy to shelve the current project that has been floundering for a few weeks and to turn your attention to the glittering new concept.

Sometimes it is tempting to convince yourself that the original book idea was flawed and that it would be much better if you took it in a completely different direction. So, your personal memoir of how you battled with chronic fatigue syndrome using alternative therapies and got your life back becomes a practical guide to using acupuncture and other complementary therapies for the treatment of CFS.

Occasionally, changing the focus of your writing project is an improvement on the original idea, but, more often than not, it is no more than a way of putting off the challenge of finishing the first book. I would not suggest for one minute that completing a book is easy – far from it. (There are techniques and tips for staying the course in Chapter 12.) However, what I would say here is that it takes effort to stay focused, but that effort is rewarded many times over if you persevere.

If you are flagging, remind yourself of what first excited you about the project; reread your original notes and the plot outline that you came up with as a result; and relive that imaginary interview in which you revealed your aims for the book, adding an answer to the question 'What obstacles did you have to overcome to finish the manuscript?' The answers you come up with may surprise you and may spontaneously supply the impetus you need to return to the project refreshed and to keep your mind focused on the finish line.

Focus points

* It helps to plan the order in which you present your information, both across the whole book (chapter breakdown) and within each chapter.

* Choose only the most powerful, persuasive and pertinent pieces of research for inclusion in your book and file the rest. If you include every piece of research you have gathered, your writing will become muddled and convoluted.

* Keep personal opinions, asides and observations away from your writing.

* Don't be tempted to make up your story as you go along. Plan the plot in advance and stick to it as far as possible.

* Keep in mind your target reader and what you want them to experience when reading your book.

* Don't get sidetracked by new and more exciting projects. Remind yourself about what first excited you regarding the ongoing book and stay the course.

Next step

In the next chapter we'll explore some of the common mistakes that writers make when it comes to developing characters and writing dialogue.

7

Characters and dialogue

In this chapter you will learn:

▶ *How to avoid stereotypical characters*
▶ *Ways to develop your characters*
▶ *How to avoid relying too heavily on description*
▶ *How to get the right tone and language for dialogue*
▶ *How dialogue can develop and show your characters.*

You may think it strange to have a whole chapter devoted to characters and dialogue, which, after all, are only facets of fiction writing. However, I have devoted this amount of space to these two topics because there is such enormous scope for getting these essential elements of fiction writing horribly wrong. So let's look at ways to avoid some of the more common pitfalls of characterization and dialogue.

Characterization

If I ask students on my writing courses about their favourite books, it is always vivid characters that they remember rather than the plot of the book. Captain Jack Aubrey in Patrick O'Brien's nautical history book series, Lisbeth Salander in Stieg Larsson's Millennium Trilogy, Ebenezer Scrooge from Dickens's *A Christmas Carol*, or Jane Austen's Elizabeth Bennet in *Pride and Prejudice* are all larger-than-life characters whom readers remember long after they have forgotten the storyline. In fact, the names of memorable characters – such as Scrooge – have even entered into the English language as words that personify the qualities they exhibited in the story, in Scrooge's case a mean-spirited miser.

So you can see how important it is to create memorable and credible characters. The problem is that most new writers are aware of this, and they then fall into the trap of trying too hard.

BELIEVABLE CHARACTERS

In an effort to make your villains more villainous and your heroes more heroic, it can be tempting to over-egg the pudding and to exaggerate the qualities associated with their role, and, as a result, your characters become far-fetched.

If you want to create believable characters, then you must avoid littering your manuscript with social stereotypes. If you populate your pages with chirpy cockneys, efficient Germans, camp homosexuals, murderous psychopaths and bitter spinsters, there will be no surprises for your readers, and you will end up with flat, one-dimensional characters that no one is interested in.

In recent years, the trend has been to create anti-heroes who are ever more shocking. So, the usual anti-establishment, maverick cop has now been ramped up a notch. For example, in the American TV series *Dexter*, he has morphed into a blood spatter pattern expert for the Miami Metro police department who, by night, is a serial killer. A fairly extreme anti-hero, you'd probably agree. In a similar vein, the central character in the detective novels by Lawrence Block is a hitman. It is quite some achievement to keep your readers on your side when your leading character is a contract killer or a serial killer.

The point is that, while it is not infeasible to make your central character unsympathetic, you are making your job much harder. Unless it is essential to the story, it is far better to make your main character likeable, albeit flawed perhaps, rather than take the risk of alienating your reader in the pursuit of ever more unlikely and extreme characterization. Keep 'em real.

Writers' top tip 25: Don't kill off your leading character

A central character who can carry a series of books gives you longevity as a writer. So you would be ill advised to kill off a good leading character at the end of your first book. It's better to find a different shock ending.

REAL PEOPLE IN FICTION

It is not uncommon for writers to use a novel to take revenge on those who have wronged them in the past by basing the nastiest character in the book on this real-life person. The problem with seeking vengeance in this way is that it can lead to litigation if the unsympathetically portrayed person feels they can be recognized from your words – you could end up in a costly libel case. There is also the issue of privacy. Anyone mentioned in the book, even if it is in a positive light, who can reasonably argue that they can be identified, could raise the legal point that it affects their privacy once it is in the public domain.

That's not to say that you cannot base characters on people whom you already know – you must simply be careful that you change enough details so that they cannot be recognized. In fact, using someone you know as the basis for a fictitious character has the advantage that you will know how your character might react in a given situation because you know how the real-life character would behave. It can inform what you do with the character.

The drawback is that it's hard to separate the real person from the character in your mind. So, if you want your character to take a course of action that would be unlikely for the real-life person, it can become problematic and limit your imagination. For example, if you have based your character on a favourite aunt and the plot requires your character to fly across the world, yet you know that Auntie hates flying, it could make you hesitate to follow that storyline.

The best solution to all this is to create composite characters based on elements from various different people. This gives you the benefit of knowing the answers to questions you might ask yourself about the character, while at the same time making them unique and unidentifiable.

Writers' top tip 26: What's in a name?

Choosing the names of the characters in your book is a wholly intuitive exercise. The right name will resonate with you and help you to better visualize your character. But bear in mind that it should be in keeping with the period in which the book is set. If you're writing a Victorian romance, the heroine is unlikely to be called Tracey, however much you love the name. If you want authentic names from a specific era, visit the local graveyard and check out the tombstones for the popular names of the time.

The threat of libel action is also a very real problem for the non-fiction writer who wants to chronicle their experiences in a memoir. Recently, I have received a lot of 'triumph over adversity' manuscripts outlining childhood abuses from authors in their 20s and 30s. The perpetrators are still alive and this poses a problem for potential publishers. There are ways around this – changing names, dates and locations – but, depending on their motives for writing the book, this is not always acceptable. Publishers are currently stringently tightening their contracts to protect themselves against libellous material in memoirs, so my advice is to write the story, changing names where possible, and then get a legal read-through before submission, if you can.

If not, you should be prepared for publishers to request a legal read before they make any judgements about the potential for publication. They may request changes at that stage, too.

Try it now: Get to know your characters

It is essential that you know your central characters intimately. To that end, it can be helpful to write a profile for each and every major character, including personal histories that take place before your story even starts (type of upbringing, etc.). Don't just stick to details about lifestyle but try to get inside their head. Ask yourself what they want from life and how they are likely to make their dreams a reality. If you can imagine your characters and how they might react in various situations outside your storyline, then this will help you to know what action and reactions are believable in your story.

DESCRIBING YOUR CHARACTER

Although it sounds straightforward to simply describe your character for your reader, this writing device is fraught with hazards and is now rather dated (it was popular with Victorian authors). Today's writers tend to prefer to show a character through their actions rather than by telling. Nonetheless, the inexperienced writer is still prone to relying too heavily on physical description, revealing every detail of the character's appearance and temperament in a great deluge as soon as the reader meets him/her. This gives you the gist:

> 'Leon was a giant of a man. He had grey eyes under a shaggy fringe of black hair, and an angry expression could be found on his craggy, stubbly face most of the time. He wore his usual faded plaid shirt with worn forest-green corduroy trousers and his father's scuffed leather belt around his huge girth...'

Rather than downloading every detail straight away, why not reveal bits of your character's appearance and personality as the book progresses? However, you should always give the reader the most salient points at the beginning – it would be mean to introduce your hero's false limb in Chapter 5, by which time the reader already has an image of him as an able-bodied fellow. This can look like changing a character just to suit the plot.

Another easy option that the inexperienced writer tends to fall back on is the use of generic adjectives for character description – words such as 'beautiful', 'handsome', 'friendly' or 'attractive'. These are not specific enough for main characters. Reserve them for more minor characters when a quick description is all that is needed.

Writers' top tip 27: The importance of place

It's not only through a description of their physical person that you get an image of a character. Your character's surroundings can give the reader a great deal of information, too. Describing the setting can be as evocative as describing the character. The Orange Prize-shortlisted writer Monique Roffey has said, 'Never underestimate the importance of place and its impact on the lives and emotions of your characters. All any novice writer needs to do is read the first chapter of *The Grapes of Wrath* to know about the importance of place in fiction.'

Try it now: People-watch

If you want inspiration for the characters in your novel, then spend time observing people. While travelling on a train, observe your fellow passengers, or sit in a café and watch who comes in and out. Imagine what their personal lives are like and ponder on how their outer appearance might feed your ideas.

SHOW, DON'T TELL

This is a well-used phrase on writing courses but it is apt nonetheless. You can avoid the temptation to tell your reader about your characters' personality and instead let their actions convey the same message. So, if you *show* me a girl at a party sitting alone, not making eye contact but watching the action avidly, you don't have to *tell* me she's under-confident and socially gauche.

Revealing character through action is just as useful for non-fiction as fiction. For example, describing someone's behaviour and actions during an interview can sometimes reveal more about that person than their words. If you reveal that an interviewee is terse with junior hotel staff and inattentive before and after the interview, these actions can belie their sugared words on tape.

CHARACTER DEVELOPMENT

In most instances, it is the characters that drive the story but characters should never be static. Your characters should develop as they progress through the book.

Whether your plot is linear (where the action moves straightforwardly, building tension until the final denouement) or cyclical (where the story follows the pattern of departure, initiation and return, such as you see in the classic adventure stories such as *The Hobbit* or the tales about King Arthur and his knights), your characters need to be changed by their adventures, and usually for the better. So, Bilbo Baggins is initially conservative and unadventurous but he meets the challenges of trolls, goblins and dragons on his journey and realizes that he has hidden depths of courage and loyalty, before returning home for tea and crumpets in his hobbit-hole.

In Hollywood love stories, the couple often hate each other initially (typically, the woman is selfish and spoiled and the man is unfeeling and brutish) and through their adventures they come to see the more genuine and caring side of the other's personality and they end up in love. It's the classic basis for films such as *Overboard*, *Crocodile Dundee*, *Mr. & Mrs. Smith*, *Star Wars*, *Indiana Jones and the Temple of Doom* and *What Happens in Vegas*. This list is endless. Most of these films are inspired by books but the all-time classic version of this 'girl hates boy, girl ends up loving boy' character development is, of course, Jane Austen's *Pride and Prejudice*.

The character arc does not have to be as pronounced as in the above examples. It can be that they simply have a new appreciation after their journey or they grow in confidence through meeting someone else (think of Kathy Bates's transformation from bored, timid housewife to feisty chick after she befriends a lively old lady in a nursing home in the comedy *Fried Green Tomatoes*), but readers like to see some kind of development or transformation in their leading characters.

Dialogue

It's very rare to find a novel or creative non-fiction that does not have conversation between the characters. Readers like conversation but the problem is that it's hard to master and the scope for getting it wrong is enormous.

Here, we'll investigate some of the more common blunders that novice writers make when writing dialogue and explore ways to avoid these pitfalls.

TRYING TO BE REAL

Real-life conversation is very different from the dialogue you read in a book. In conversation, we jump about, we don't finish sentences and our meaning is always informed by our facial expressions, gestures and intonation.

In dialogue we have none of the visual aids. A good example of how written English varies from spoken English is an email exchange. There is no nuance by email, so a conversation can easily 'flame' and escalate into bad feeling if meaning is misunderstood.

Although written dialogue has to feel like spoken conversation, it doesn't have to mimic our rambling, disconnected speech. If you're after realism, you can convey that by use of language but, for heaven's sake, leave out the 'umms', 'ers' and anything else that will leave your reader feeling bored.

The converse of this common mistake is to make dialogue unnaturally good. In your head your character's superbly witty, grammatically perfect speech may sound amazing, but to your reader it will sound false and will be more likely to irritate than impress.

EXPOSITION

Dialogue is active. That is to say, it *shows* the character in action rather than you *telling* the reader about him or her. In this way, you can use dialogue to develop your characters. It is a great way to help the reader learn more about them and what makes them tick.

Unfortunately, it is easy to get carried away with the idea of revealing things about a character through dialogue, by having one character telling another a piece of information that they would never realistically need to give them. Avoid the scenario of: 'I've just seen Rosalind, your best friend who is married to James, the banker. Did you know she was in town?'

Writers' top tip 28: Use a walk-on character for exposition

Experienced writers have always used characters whose role offers them a legitimate reason to ask questions. So doctors, police officers, journalists, etc. often appear in order to create a dialogue that provides all the information the reader needs to know. If you don't have a handy official in your plot, a meddling neighbour or curious friend can also serve the same purpose.

HE SAID / SHE SAID

This is one of the most common mistakes that novice novel writers make. The prolific use of 'he said' / 'she said' at the end of every line of dialogue is unnecessary when there are only two voices in the conversation. Credit your reader with enough sense to be able to work out that, when one character stops speaking, it is the other person in the conversation who replies. If there are more than two people conversing, then the occasional reference to who is speaking, just to avoid any confusion, is fine. And if you want to escape the whole, 'said John', 'said Emma', 'said John', 'said Rachel', 'said Emma', 'said John' scenario, then you can always break up the dialogue by using an extending sentence that adds description. For example: 'My goodness, I've never seen such a big cat,' said Emma, as she picked up the ginger tom that had been winding around her legs.

In an attempt to avoid the first hazard of 'he said' / 'she said' dialogue, many inexperienced writers resort to using synonyms for 'said'. In truth, this is even worse. A manuscript strewn with 'he exclaimed', 'she protested', 'demanded Alan', 'retorted Melanie', 'he cried out', 'she whimpered' and their ilk simply looks amateurish.

SETTINGS

It can be helpful to the reader to know where the conversation is taking place, so they can picture the scene. You don't have to spell it out in detail; little hints while the dialogue is going on are helpful. You can also use the setting to reveal more of the speakers' emotions behind their words. So, if a self-absorbed husband is telling his wife about his new and very attractive young secretary while sunning himself on a lounger in the garden, her pruning action on the roses may become more aggressive as she feigns nonchalance but feels anger welling up inside her.

DIALECT

Most writers know that it is important to give each character a distinctive voice, and you may be tempted by this to give a character a Geordie or a Rasta accent, for example, to make them more interesting. Here, you are verging into dangerous territory because it is notoriously hard to write in dialect and to make it work. If you are wholly familiar with the dialect and can use the right turn of phrase and expressions, you may get away with it but you must still bear in mind that your reader may well be from a different region/location and will struggle to sound the sentences in his or her head. So, unless it's essential to the plot, it's probably best to avoid dialects altogether.

Remember this: Don't use swearing gratuitously

Swearing is much more commonplace now and it may seem strange if some characters do not swear in dialogue. Nonetheless, use profanity with careful thought – swearing in the written word has a much greater impact than when spoken.

LAYOUT

How dialogue appears in your manuscript is another area that catches out the unwary writer. I imagine I've seen every conceivable variation on the presentation of dialogue – from running it on in the main text to using different coloured type for every participant in the conversation – but I may yet be surprised by another variation on the theme.

In fact, the layout for dialogue is straightforward if you remember the few simple rules we've already looked at in Chapter 4. As a refresher...

▶ You start each person's speech on a new line.

▶ Use either double (favoured in the USA) or single (favoured in the UK) quotation marks – it doesn't matter, but be consistent.

▶ If a speech runs over more than one paragraph, you do not use closed quotation marks at the end of a paragraph until the speech ends, but you use open quotation marks at the beginning of every paragraph within the speech. (That said, as a generalization, no character should speak for more than about three or four lines of typing without other characters coming in. We are trying to avoid the Shakespearean-style soliloquy, remember.)

Writers' top tip 29: The point of dialogue...

Written dialogue must feel like real conversation but its purpose is also to:
* move the story forward
* reveal more of the character
* stick to the point
* be interesting
* be reasonably brief (three or four lines at most)
* make sense to the reader.

Try it now: Get a feel for good dialogue

Practice is the only way to get the hang of writing dialogue. So write down conversations that you've overheard that amuse you; listen to radio plays; pay attention to dialogue in the books that you read – what works and what doesn't. Become aware of the spoken word and how it translates into writing.

Case study: Dorothy Lumley, proprietor of the Dorian Literary Agency, which specializes in fiction

'You've probably come across the phrases "character led" as opposed to "plot driven" when describing novels. While both are equally valid, people have a preference for one or the other, both as writers and readers. I have a preference for character-led novels and have sometimes turned down material because I felt it was more about the ideas than the characters. That's not to say there's anything wrong with that – it's just what I happen to like.'

▶ On the opening chapter

'Ideally, a novel should be a good balance of character and plot. Drawing the reader into caring about the central character(s) and the dilemmas you throw at them makes a novel more compelling. Here are some tips for that opening chapter – bearing in mind that, as with all tips, a great writer can break all the rules!

✳ Avoid starting with a minor character, or someone who dies within the first few pages. (Yes, people do do that! And I always feel cheated.)

✳ Show, don't tell. In other words, allow the characters themselves to reveal their thoughts and feelings. Stay inside their minds and hearts. Don't be the novelist telling us about them and what's happening.

✳ Avoid potted biographies and also long flashbacks at this early point. Stay in the moment and drip-feed important facts in gradually, arising out of dialogue and characters' thoughts.

✳ Don't hide information or hold things back, thinking this will increase suspense. It does the opposite. The more you reveal about what your character is facing, the better, whether the conflicts/threats are of an internal nature, from other characters, or outside historical/physical events. Tension builds as we see how they deal with what you throw at them.'

▶ On irresistible characters

'Many experienced writers compose detailed character studies of their main characters (two or three really central characters, with a maximum of six – too many characters can be confusing). They create a biography covering everything from schooldays to star sign and surface traits as well as deeper motivation, in addition to physical description. They may not use all this information in the novel, but simply knowing it makes the character more real.

'The first step, therefore, whether you write it down or keep it in your head, is to really get to know your character(s) well so that they come alive on the page, bringing credibility and authenticity.

'A character flaw can be very engaging. How often have we come across a headstrong person who we can see heading for disaster due to pride, stubbornness or anger, for example, and wanted to shout at them "Stop!" We have to keep turning the pages to find out how they deal with what happens after their fall. Or will they realize their mistakes in time?

'To use that dreaded word, the central character is on a "journey". They should ideally grow and change through the novel and the ending should have a satisfying, rounded feel that feels "right". I was disturbed by the ending of *The Killing* when I felt Detective Lund acted right out of character – I felt the producers had a clever shocking idea but I didn't think it fitted with the integrity of the character I'd come to know. I wonder what actress Sofie Gråbøl thought? I'd love to know!'

▶ On plot development

'Tips on improving plotting run somewhat parallel to those on character:

✳ Exposition – give the reader a feel for the tone of the novel (humorous/dark/romantic/horror/historical, etc.) on page 1.

✳ My advice would be that, if you are not yet published, you should stick closely to the conventions of genre in the early novels – start to experiment later. For example, get the dead body on the page as close to the beginning in a crime novel. Hero and heroine should meet on page 1 or as close as, in a romance, and be interacting together for 75 per cent of the time in a traditional romance.

✳ As for character – don't hide or hold back, but give as much away as possible in order to develop the plot and get the reader interested.

Everyone has their own way of working. I find working on chapter breakdowns helpful. I work out how many chapters I'm going to use, list them, then put in each chapter the key scenes I think should be there, which should push forward either character or plot, or both. Some authors have a board with lots of sticky notes, cards, all sorts of ideas that will need to be put in. Others will have long charts running around their office walls, especially for long complicated historical novels, to keep a track of their timelines and plot.

And here are some pointers on getting the plot flow right:

* To keep the pace moving, plunge straight into the middle of the next scene – there's no need to lead up to it.

* When looking at your flow chart or chapter breakdown, work in highs and lows so that the mood alters. There should be quieter interludes before something high-octane happens – though towards the denouement it's often a case of building tension on tension.

* To borrow a phrase from the movies – up the ante! Whenever the central character seems to be finding a way to resolve their problems, something even worse should befall them until, just when you think everything is completely stacked against them, there's a final twist in which they manage to resolve everything, with or without the help of outside forces.

* Keep a close eye on your timeline and continuity.

* Avoid rushing the ending. Make sure it has that satisfying rounded feel, though you don't need to tie up every loose end.'

Focus points

* Make characters believable but show them warts and all.
  Unsympathetic lead characters are hard to portray successfully.
* Be wary of portraying characters based on real people as there may be
  legal repercussions.
* Disclose descriptions of your characters gradually through the opening
  chapters.
* Reveal personality through a character's actions rather than telling
  the reader.
* Dialogue needs to feel like conversation, but should not mimic it.
* Be frugal with the use of 'he said' etc. when writing dialogue but avoid
  using alternative verbs.

Next step

**We will now turn our attention to ways to make
your book a more appealing option to prospective
agents and publishers by making sure it is
marketable.**

8

Is your book marketable?

In this chapter you will learn:

▶ *How to give your book the best chance of publishing success*
▶ *What publishers are looking for*
▶ *Ways to come up with an original angle*
▶ *Ways to manage your credibility as an author.*

The title of this chapter is not a question that is at the forefront of your mind when you are writing your book perhaps, but it is one that you must at some point address if you want to improve your chances of getting published.

And there are two main bones of contention with marketability, particularly when talking about popular non-fiction books. The first point is that it does not matter how interesting your views, how important the message you are imparting, or how well placed and well qualified you are to write your book, if you cannot make your subject accessible to a mass audience – and by that I mean if you are not able to write in a popular style – your book will not find its way on to the bookshelves.

What is harder for an author to accept – and I have witnessed plenty of new writers who are incredulous when I give them this feedback on their manuscripts – is that the converse is also true. Namely, that it can be the best written, most beautifully crafted and entertaining book in the world, but if there is no audience for a title on this particular subject, and there is not enough public interest, no publisher will take you on.

I accept that this is quite a hard thing to hear when you have so lovingly produced a work of great writing, but the end product must be marketable. Thankfully, the first mistake of not writing in a popular style is, to some extent, surmountable – you could take a writing course, get a writing coach or give greater attention to loosening up and polishing your style. However, the second problem of lack of audience is not one that can be so easily overcome.

When I was asked to edit an online magazine website for the over-50s back in the early 1990s, it looked like a very promising project. The publisher had spotted a growing market of an ageing but fit population, but, sadly, we were ahead of our time and the project folded after about a year. Now, of course, there are countless online sites and magazines for the silver surfer. The same principle applies to books. You have to catch the power wave – if you are too far ahead or behind it, then your book – however good it might be – is unlikely to find a publisher.

What sets your book apart?

So, how can you identify whether there is an audience for your proposed book? (And I recommend that you look into this before you spend countless hours labouring over your manuscript.) First, check to see whether there are any books already on the market on your chosen subject – that is the first gauge of whether or not you have an audience, and perhaps the most persuasive indicator for traditional book publishers. Nonetheless, even if there are no competitive titles on Amazon, for example, you can look to see if there are any courses on the subject that would indicate that it is growing in popularity. What about magazines? Are there any national members' clubs in your specialist field with good membership figures? These can all give an indication to a prospective publisher that there is a market, even if it has not yet been targeted by a book.

Please do not take this as encouragement to over-egg the size of your prospective audience in your book proposal. That is actually another common mistake that you should definitely avoid. For example, any publisher will see straight through a statement along the lines of 'My book is an unofficial biography of Walter da Silva, the chief designer for Audi. The number of cars on the world's roads surpassed one billion in 2010, so there is a limitless audience for my book.' That sort of illogical, sweeping statement is not going to wash. Be realistic in your estimates of the potential audience for your book but show that you have researched the market sensibly – members' clubs are viable audiences for a specialist book.

There are other ways that you can look at how to improve the marketability and viability of both your book and yourself, as the author. Let's take a look.

Writers' top tip 30: Make your work accessible

You must be able to make your writing accessible to a mass audience.

Writers' top tip 31: Make sure there's a market

No matter how good your book is, if a publisher cannot identify a market for it, they will not take it on.

Originality

The famous designer Marcel Wander once said, 'Everything has been done. There are no new ideas left. Whatever we can think of … has been done before.' Whether you subscribe to that view or not, it's a pretty fair bet that when you are writing a popular or technical subject-led non-fiction book, there are likely to be books already in the market on that topic. And if it's a perennially popular subject, there will be literally hundreds of books on the subject in print.

The good thing about this is that you do not have to persuade a prospective publisher of the existing audience for your book. However, where many new writers go wrong is that they simply want to write about a subject that is close to their heart without giving due thought to what makes their book sufficiently different from the competition.

Remember this: A brief window of opportunity

A prospective buyer in a bookshop will look at the front cover, the back cover blurb and possibly the list of contents and he or she may flick through a couple of pages. That short window of opportunity is all that you have to persuade him or her to buy your book rather than a competitor title, so it is imperative that your unique angle is obvious enough to convince them that this is the right book for them.

The fact is that you have to find an angle from which to approach the topic that is original. In journalistic terms, you are looking for 'the hook'. In plain English, that translates into: How does your book stand out from the crowd? What makes it special?

It is not enough to say that your voice alone is what makes it special. That will not cut any ice with a publisher. If there is nothing to distinguish your book from the countless others, many of which come with the added advantage of a high-profile author or a celebrity endorsement, it is highly unlikely that it will be picked up.

You need to identify a new and original angle for the topic. If this is not making much sense to you, let's look at the example of *Men Are from Mars, Women Are from Venus*

(HarperCollins, 1992), a book written by the American author and relationship counsellor John Gray. The book has sold more than 50 million copies and, according to CNN, was the 'highest ranked work of nonfiction' of the 1990s, spending 121 weeks on the bestseller list. It certainly was not the first book to be published on the differences between the sexes (in fact, they were plentiful), but the angle that men and women are so different that they might as well come from different planets was completely original. It was a concept that people could grasp straight away. It was his unique approach to a well-worn subject that helped to make his book successful.

Try it now: Research your competitors

If you already have a book idea in mind, do some background research on its marketability. Make a list of competitor titles already on sale and then make a list of what makes your book different. Find your angle, and if you can't come up with something, then perhaps it's not such a strong idea as you at first imagined.

Writers' top tip 32 : Assess your competitors' strengths and weaknesses

Looking at the strengths and weaknesses of similar titles on the market will give some indication of how you can make your book unique.

Title

Let's be honest, no publisher in his right mind is going to turn down your book simply because it has a bad title. Nonetheless, a well-thought-out title that captures the flavour of the book and the fashion of the moment can go a long way towards persuading a publisher that you know what will work for your kind of reader. The current vogue in non-fiction publishing is for a snappy, eye-catching heading with an explanatory strapline underneath, such as Maria Landon's *Daddy's Little Earner: A heartbreaking true story of a brave little girl's escape from violence* (Harper Element, 2008).

Author credibility

Often, writers think that, once they have written the book, the writing will speak for itself and that will be enough. That might have been the case once upon a time, but in the age of social media where everyone has an identity, a publisher looks at the whole package and authors cannot be found wanting.

First, you have to have the right credentials, as we discussed in Chapter 5. It is a given that you can write in an engaging, popular style, but you have to also have some qualifications or experiential credentials that make you the ideal candidate to write the book. So, to pen a guide on relationships, it would be useful if you were a practising couples' counsellor, psychotherapist, psychiatrist or sociologist. It is not enough to say that you have had a lot of boyfriends/girlfriends and are speaking from experience.

You may have noticed that I said 'practising' specialist. If you retired from practice five years ago to concentrate on your writing career, a publisher may feel that your expertise is somewhat out of date. They want authors with their fingers on the pulse so that the reader feels they are getting cutting-edge advice.

Similarly, if you are still in practice or running workshops, there is a good chance that you will have a network of clients and supporters. Although not crucial, it is important to publishers that potential authors have what's known in the trade as a 'platform', namely a way to reach an audience that is already persuaded of their merits and loyal to their work. Workshop lists, social media connections and followers – it is all grist to the mill as far as a publisher is concerned.

There are other ways to make yourself more marketable if you don't have relevant credentials or a sizeable platform. Perhaps you could look at creating an alter ego – a different persona from the everyday person that you are, one that is a catchy hook for the media. A good case in point is the UK newspaper journalist Susie Boniface. She had bylines in the national press that had largely gone unnoticed for 18 years. It was only when she started a pseudonymous blog about her husband's affair and her marriage break-up that she gained notoriety, and a book deal with Constable & Robinson followed. As the woman behind

@fleetstreetfox, her blog has been read by millions and more than 52,000 people follow her tweets every day. Excerpts from her book *The Diaries of a Fleet Street Fox: The Truest Tabloid Tale You'll Ever Read,* were printed in *The Times*. If she had written the same book before her incarnation as the Fleet Street Fox, it is questionable whether she would have got the publishing deal – it certainly would not have been such a generous one.

Writers' top tip 33: Invent a persona

Don't be afraid to change your name to a pen name if it is a better fit for the target audience or a catchy hook for the media.

Perhaps a blog dishing the dirt on tabloid scandals may sound a bit out of your league, but do not dismiss the idea of using a pseudonym out of hand. If you know your market, then you will know what sort of pen name will sit comfortably with them. If your given name is a bad match with the genre of writing of your choice and its audience expectations, then why not choose a pseudonym? As Roger Thistlethwaite, you may not feel best placed to write a bodice-ripping historical love story, so become someone else. As you know, I wrote the boys' survival guides as the adventure-loving author Rory Storm. That is because most 12-year-old boys would not want to hear tales of derring-do from down-to-earth Claire Gillman. The books have been successful, but I doubt whether any of the readers would want to know that the author was actually a middle-aged woman!

Try it now: Invent some pen names

Think of various different genres and come up with a selection of appropriate pen names for each. You can have some fun with this... How about a travel guide by Sergio Roamin, or a romantic novel by Venus Huggins? Enjoy!

Positioning

Once again, we come back to a variation on a theme that we first mentioned in Chapter 5, and that is where your book will be positioned on the shelves One of the major failings of the manuscripts that I review is not understanding that your book will be pigeon-holed into a genre or subcategory of a genre and must therefore comply with expectations of a book of that particular style. I am not suggesting for one minute that you should lose the passion you have to tell a story or to share a subject, but modern authors need to keep a weather-eye on how the product of their labours will be sold. Where will it sit on the shelves? And does your book fulfil the brief of that genre?

A self-help or how-to guide needs to have a large proportion of practical advice, popular fiction must be engaging and entertaining, a memoir should be a personal account of events or a period in your life. All these are straightforward requirements of the genre.

The problem arises when there is crossover between genres. For example, what if you write about your battles with prescription drug addiction and share the ways that you overcame it – is that a memoir or a self-help guide? If you write about an historical event with real-life characters but you put views and words in the mouths of your characters, is that a historical novel or a piece of creative non-fiction?

In fact, creative non-fiction has become a hugely popular genre in its own right, thanks in large measure to the success of books like Antony Beevor's *Stalingrad* and Hilary Mantel's *Wolf Hall*. Both authors have looked at actual events and periods of history but have in part told the tale using the voice of the common man or the ordinary soldier and a supporting cast of fictional characters.

As to the other genres, you must try to make sure your book does not fall between two stools, so to speak. Decide whether it is a memoir or a motivational self-help book and then put the emphasis on that angle. You are then able to describe your book in those terms in your proposal – 'This is a self-help book that has the additional benefit of anecdotal material from my own life experiences.'

Writing to length

Yet again, this is a consideration that will not be at the forefront of your mind; nonetheless, if you are aware that certain genres of book are usually published at fairly standard lengths, then you will increase your chances of success if you produce a manuscript that is close to that figure. That is not to say that a well-written book that is wide of the word count will not be accepted, but it is that hoary old chestnut again – it is more marketable if it conforms to standard expectations, so why not give yourself the best shot?

With that in mind, let me outline here the usual lengths of manuscripts within the specialist genres.

A potential publisher is looking for a work of fiction between 70,000 to 150,000 words, so if your manuscript is very wide of this mark, be it too long or too short, you are compromising your chances of acceptance. The exception to the rule is adult fantasy or science fiction which is notoriously weighty, so there you can aim for the top end of the word count range. For all other fiction, aim for somewhere in the region of 90,000 to 120,000 words. If your manuscript is much longer than this, would your book be more marketable as two volumes or as a trilogy rather than as a single book?

Obviously, children's books are usually shorter than adult novels because most children do not have the same attention span or reading skills as adults. So you would be looking at an early reader book of around 2,500 words, a chapter book of around 6,000 to 10,000 words, and a book for teens around the 40,000-word mark.

Non-fiction has a broader remit, and occasionally a publisher will accept a very thin volume on a specialist topic, so you'd be looking at 30,000 words. However, as a general rule of thumb, a popular or subject-led non-fiction book should have a word count of around 50,000 to 60,000 words.

Clearly, there are exceptions to these rules. If the rock group Queen had been bound by convention we would never have had the amazing 'Bohemian Rhapsody', which, at nearly six minutes long, was almost twice the length of a normal single record of the time. Nonetheless, there are certain expectations with regard to length of manuscript and, if you meet them, you are less likely to be rejected than if you flout them.

Case study: Kirsty Dunseath, Fiction Publishing Director, Weidenfeld & Nicolson

'As we head into 2013 I think it is quite exciting to watch the way the market is evolving. Yes, there are various issues we all have to confront, but what is clear is that the desire to find good stories is as alive and healthy as ever. And that's what you always want to find as an editor – a story that completely consumes you and makes you want to read into the small hours, whether it be on paper, on a Kindle, on a smartphone or tablet (or whatever other medium is dreamed up this year).

'It will be interesting to see how long the *Fifty Shades* phenomenon lasts. And what comes next after vampires – werewolves, ghosts, zombies...? Also, the increasing e-reader market seems to be breathing new life into the novella and short story form, as what might not be cost effective in print form can work and find an audience electronically.

'At Weidenfeld & Nicolson we are starting the year off with a bang – the paperback publication of Gillian Flynn's brilliant novel *Gone Girl*, which has already been a phenomenal bestseller in the US. We have some wonderful debuts coming up over the year, including *The Honey Guide* by Richard Crompton, *The Puppet Boy of Warsaw* by Eva Weaver and *Children of the Jacaranda Tree* by Sahar Delijani. All of these take the reader to a different time and place (Nairobi in the run-up to the 2007 elections; the Warsaw ghetto; post-revolutionary Iran), and all three have unique voices.

'There is no formula to what will make a bestseller and often it is the books that are a bit left-field that reach the charts, but what I would say is that good storytelling never goes out of fashion and that the debut novels that have publishers foaming at the mouth always have a very individual voice, strong characters and a momentum that sweeps you up in the plot and doesn't let go. So here's to finding more of that.'

For more views on what fiction editors want, go to literary agent Andrew Lownie's website: www.andrewlownie.co.uk

Remember this: How it works

Once your manuscript has been given the thumbs-up by the publisher's reader (the first hurdle), it must then convince a team of people of its worth. It is no longer the case that, if an editor loves a book, it is automatically a done deal. All manuscripts must now go before an acquisitions committee involving sales and marketing personnel as well as the editors, and possibly members of the senior management team too, and everyone must agree that this is a marketable project. These are people who know the industry extremely well, so your manuscript must tick all the boxes and appeal on every front – not just on the quality of the writing alone.

Focus points

* Give thought to what makes your book stand out from the competition.
* Look for an original angle or hook.
* A catchy title can be a bonus.
* Use a pen name if it is more appropriate for the genre.
* Make sure your book can be clearly categorized. If it is something of a hybrid, then pick the strongest genre and use the other as a marketing tool (e.g. self-help guide with personal anecdotes).
* Be aware of the usual length for the genre you're working in.

Next step

The next chapter looks at how bringing your book out at the right time to catch the Zeitgeist or the enthusiasm generated by a special event or anniversary makes good marketing sense and can optimize your chances of getting your manuscript accepted.

9

Good timing

In this chapter you will learn:

▶ *How publishers schedule publication dates*
▶ *How to use anniversaries and forthcoming events to your advantage*
▶ *About the importance of book fairs*
▶ *To factor in enough time to meet delivery deadlines and to schedule successfully.*

Now that you are confident that there is a flourishing market for your book, and your manuscript and proposal are in the best possible condition they can be, there is one further benefit of having insider knowledge of the publishing industry that you can turn to your advantage.

As a magazine and book editor, I see so many good ideas go to waste because writers simply do not understand how long the lead-in times are to produce publications. Just as an example, in January this year (and every year, I have to say) I received a plethora of feature ideas for gifts or activities for Valentine's Day (14 February). One month's notice would be stretching it for a weekly magazine, but for a bi-monthly such as *Kindred Spirit* magazine this was ludicrous; we were putting the finishing touches to the March/April issue at that time and starting to receive commissioned copy for the May/June issue. For a good Valentine's idea to be accepted for a monthly or bi-monthly magazine, the writer should have contacted us in November.

The same holds true for books. Novice writers invariably underestimate the time between the publisher commissioning or accepting a manuscript and the book's publication. This can easily be anywhere from a year to 18 months, or more, depending on the complexity of the book, the resources available to the publisher, and the needs of the market. Naturally, if a publisher wishes to rush out a time-sensitive book in response to a news event, this can happen, but it is only viable in exceptional circumstances and a normal scheduled rush job would be closer to seven months.

Book production schedules

For those lucky enough to have their manuscripts accepted, it can be a very unsettling period as they wait to see their book appear in print. Do not be overly anxious – it is normal for the process to take some considerable time, even for big-name writers.

The reason for the long wait is that, even before your manuscript is edited, copyedited, proofread and indexed, the sales and marketing teams are gearing up. It is their job to try to persuade retail buyers to get excited about your book.

Meanwhile, the retail buyers are deciding how many copies to buy and whether to put your book on promotion, perhaps on the 'three for two' tables or a front-of-the-store display, if your publisher is prepared to pay dearly.

Chain bookstores, such as Waterstones and WHSmith in the UK and Barnes & Noble in the United States, and supermarket book buyers generally buy books at least six months before the publication date. They base their estimates for how many copies of a title to order on the expected media attention and the author's sales track record, if he or she is previously published. This can make it hard for the mid-list author whose sales are steady but unremarkable. It's one of the rare occasions where it is actually an advantage to be an untested first-time author.

Writers' top tip 34: Allow plenty of lead-in time

Although digitization has made the production and printing process much faster, the whole publishing process from start to finish still takes time. So, if you have a book idea that is planned to coincide with a forthcoming event or anniversary, make sure you allow plenty of time to sell your idea and for the production and distribution process. I recommend you allow two years' lead-in time.

Book fairs

Book fairs are major events in the publishing world calendar. Publishers, agents, distributors and retailers all attend so that they can conduct business on a face-to-face basis and make contacts. There is always a huge buzz of frenetic activity in publishing houses leading up to these events, as the editors prepare proposals to gauge responses from potential co-edition publishers and for overseas sales. In fact, rights trading probably forms the main business of book fairs.

The major book fairs for UK publishers are Frankfurt, held in October, and London, held in mid-April. BookExpo America, held in early June and alternating between New York and other US cities, is the primary event for US publishers, although many British and European publishers attend to showcase their new publications to the US book trade and to meet US publishers on home territory.

Both literary agents and staff from the publishers attend book fairs armed with information and dummy material (known in the trade as a blad), both for existing and potentially forthcoming projects. Meetings between buyers and sellers usually start with a discussion about outstanding business, followed by a presentation of new projects. Although publishing business is conducted all year round, the major rights trading takes place at book fairs because so much of it depends on personal relationships, knowledge of the taste of the potential buyers and face-to-face discussions.

Literary agents, editors and publishing rights staff begin work on book fairs early and plan appointments well in advance of the event itself. Given the importance of book fairs, it would make perfect sense for you (or your agent) to get your proposal to a potential publisher in good time for the next major book fair. If they like your proposal, they may well ask you to give them some sample material for a blad, which typically consists of a cover, an introduction, two sample spreads, and back cover information. You will, of course, be paid for the work involved, but should the proposal be successful, this amount may be taken out of your advance.

Getting your proposal to publishers during the crucial run-up period can be vital. Even if you are not asked for blad copy, publishers and literary agents may well have your proposal either to hand or in mind when they go to a fair, just in case an opportunity arises. Why miss a golden opportunity like that for the sake of poor timing in submitting your proposal?

Book fairs can also be useful places for any new author to network and learn to navigate the publishing industry. At the London Book Fair, for example, there is an Author Lounge where you can gain valuable advice on all aspects of self-publishing, from writing and editing to design and marketing. Fairs also host a wide range of seminars and events, often featuring celebrated authors, which will offer inspiration and ideas for authors of all levels, but especially if you are looking to get your first book published. If you can bear the crush and the cost of entry – for the London Book Fair somewhere in the region of £50 – then it can be a worthwhile experience for the novice writer to get a flavour of the industry.

Case study: Fox & Howard Literary Agency

'Book fairs are useful to agents because they provide an opportunity to meet with our sub-agents, both to learn about what is happening in their territories (what's selling, etc.) and to check how previous submissions are faring. Obviously, it is also an opportunity to bring them up to speed on any new proposals you might have. Publishing is very much about relationships and these have to be nurtured, so many see it as an opportunity to catch up with old friends.

'Agents and publishers will usually start setting up their meetings a couple of months ahead of the fairs. Submitting a proposal to your agent a week ahead of the event is leaving it too late, as the material may not be appropriate for the publishers they have arranged to meet up with.

'It can be a useful exercise for authors to attend book fairs in terms of checking what is being published in their area of interest. However, some authors who have attended off their own bat report that they have found the experience quite dispiriting, as the sheer scale of the fairs can be intimidating. Publishers are there to sell their lists to international markets and the stands are usually manned by sales/rights staff whose diaries are filled with back-to-back meetings. Authors trying to sell their books will usually be told to approach editorial staff back at HQ.

'Where attending a book fair can be more useful from an author's point of view is for the specialist knowledge that you can pick up. All of the bigger international fairs such as New York, London and Frankfurt host many specialist talks on diverse subjects from literary trends to learning about developments in emerging markets such as Brazil. There are also talks on new technology and digital publishing .This is very useful for agents but also for aspiring authors.

'There are many literary festivals held across the country and perhaps these present authors with more useful opportunities than the big book fairs. They are on a smaller scale, frequently specialist and there are many more authors in attendance who might well be happy to take time out to chat with their peers and compare notes.'

Writers' top tip 35: Get your timing right

The period after a book fair is usually extremely busy, as rights sellers, agents and editors follow up on leads made at the fair, confirming what has been agreed, drawing up contracts, and providing information or sample material that may have been promised. If you did not manage to submit your proposal in good time for a book fair, it is advisable to leave it for some weeks after the event, otherwise it can easily get lost in all the commotion, or dismissed without due consideration.

Literary festivals

I have been lucky enough to be invited to speak at various literary festivals including Malfest, and so I know that festivals can be a great place for authors to network and to get a greater feel for the industry. They tend to be less frenetic than the book fairs, and professionals who are there either as speakers or stallholders (authors often attend to sell their books directly to their readers) seem to have more time and a more relaxed attitude to meeting would-be authors. In the Q&A sessions you can learn a great deal, even if you do not ask a question yourself, as the issues vexing new writers tend to be commonly shared.

Try it now: Make time for a book festival

There are countless literary festivals all over the world. They are a great way to hear from professional authors, to get a feel for the business and possibly to make some useful contacts. Check out the dates for the nearest major event to you and go along.

Looking forward

For non-fiction authors, a publisher is more likely to take an interest in your book proposal if there is an anniversary or important date or event that coincides with its publication that will be a 'hook' for media attention and public interest.

For example, in 2012 publishers scheduled a range of titles to coincide with the London Olympics, including Peter Ackroyd's biography of the city of London, eponymously entitled *London*, John Every's *The Green London Way*, which uncovers green spaces in the city, and *India's Olympic Story*, drawing attention to the place of Indian athletes in this global sporting event.

Looking forward, 2015 will be the 200th anniversary of the Battle of Waterloo. There will obviously be a plethora of military histories published to coincide with this important anniversary, not to mention biographies of Wellington, but the link can be fairly tenuous – perhaps a local history on Stratfield Saye House (Wellington's family seat) and its environs might interest a publisher if you tie the book into the upcoming anniversary of Wellington's biggest victory.

The links are less obvious for fiction writers but they are there nonetheless. At the time of the Beijing Olympics in 2008, Penguin published *Wolf Totem*, a novel by Jiang Rong, to coincide with the event, and that went on to win the Man Asia Literary Prize. If there is a major election coming up, a novel set in the world of politics might be an attractive proposition.

The other side of this marketing coin is that around the time of US presidential elections, for example, non-fiction political titles will probably sell well but other titles may suffer. Publishers no longer rely on book reviews for sales, but they know that, in the election season, only political titles will get coverage in the book pages and on radio and television. The same media that can call attention to a book at the right time can also draw readers' attention away from it at the wrong time.

If you do decide to use an impending anniversary or date as a marketing incentive in your proposal to a potential agent or publisher, bear in mind that books need a long schedule between commissioning and publication, so give yourself (and the publisher) plenty of time to write, produce and publish the book in time for the anniversary.

Remember this: Help out the publicity department

Weeks before the publication date of your book, the publisher's publicity department will be targeting magazine editors and radio/television producers to try to persuade them to interview you or to serialize your book. Any help you can give them with unusual angles will help enormously.

Try it now: Do a lecture series

If you have written about a local history event to coincide with an anniversary, for example, it will help your book a great deal if you are able to do a lecture series or local tour that the publisher's marketing department could use to good effect for publicity. Scout out local church groups, women's clubs, servicemen's clubs and local bookstores that might be willing to host a talk.

The right time to publish

Publishers have preferred times of the year for publishing books. If you are accepted by a commercial publisher, you will probably have no say in the publication date of your book, which is governed by production milestones and the schedules of the other books on their list. However, if you are self-publishing or working with a small independent publisher, then you might like to give thought to the publication date, as you should have some say in it.

Most genres of books are published in the early autumn as this gives booksellers time to stock the title before the Christmas rush. It also means that your title is not competing with the celebrity big-sellers which weigh down the bookshelves in the run-up to Christmas. Business books also sell well in the early-autumn months as they capitalize on the 'back to school' mentality.

Naturally, you too can profit from the Christmas season if yours is a coffee-table book, a novel or a big biography, as all of these do well as gifts. If you are publishing an e-book, a December publication date might mean you can cash in on the enthusiasm of those who receive e-readers/tablets for Christmas and who may well be surfing for new authors. The flipside of this is that there is more competition from widespread Christmas gift promotions than usual.

Writers' top tip 36: January publication

It may seem odd but a book published in late December has a shorter shelf life than if you postpone things for a week or so and publish on 2 January the following year. It's a trick of the mind, but a fact of life.

You can publish self-help, fitness/health and diet titles in December ready for the January promotions, which often start in the Boxing Day sales or shortly thereafter, as many people are thinking of a fresh start at the beginning of the new year. Meanwhile, the summer months are a good publishing window for all genres in digital book format, but for fiction in particular, as travellers like to browse the e-book outlets for their holiday reading before they set off on a trip.

Although there are advantages to publishing at certain times of the year or to coincide with a special forthcoming calendar date, it is not something to focus on too closely, especially if you are going down the traditional publishing route with a commercial publisher. Even with self-publishing, if you have the right content, a good platform to promote it and a marketing push behind it, you have every reason to hope that your book will do well whatever time of year it is published.

Remember this: Publish print and digital simultaneously

For a time many publishers staggered the release date of print and digital editions, but it is now generally accepted that simultaneous publication of print and digital editions is the gold standard. This holds true if you are self-publishing. Publish simultaneously and remember that in order to take advantage of the pre-order system for e-books on Amazon, you need to make sure the e-book is ready on the scheduled date, as failure to do so results in a black mark against the author's (and/or publisher's) name.

Delivery deadlines

As we have seen, the schedule for commercial book publishing is worked out well in advance so that the sales team have plenty of time to get books sold into the retailers and for promotions and so forth to be arranged.

If an author is late with a deadline and misses the target publication date, the stores simply do not have the room on their shelves to accommodate late books, as they are expecting next month's crop of projected bestsellers. Unless you are a major author, you may well have to wait a further four to six months to get your book published if you deliver late, largely so that a new slot can be negotiated with retailers.

You may be thinking that this does not tally with the (long out-of-date) image you have of a 'gentleman's industry' where deadlines are something of a formality and authors don't have to worry about handing in their manuscripts on time. That may have been the case back in the 'golden age' of publishing but it no longer holds true.

Not only can late delivery affect your publication date, but it can hit you in the pocket too. As publishing houses look for ways to cut costs, many literary agents report that they are holding authors to deadlines and using lateness as an opportunity to renegotiate advances. In some worst-case scenarios, they are even terminating contracts altogether.

In reality, most editors give their full support to the books they have commissioned and they want them to do well. The best thing you can do if you are having problems with delivery deadlines is to be honest with your editor about your lack of progress sooner rather than later. In this way, the editor can adjust the schedule – trimming bits off other phases of the production programme – and still bring your book in on time.

It is far better to be collaborative and to keep your editor in the picture so that they know what is going on and can help you. But what often happens is that, when an inexperienced author realizes they are going to be late delivering copy, they hide. And that's exactly the wrong thing to do.

This is why it is advisable to wait until you have finished your manuscript before seeking a book deal. Alternatively, schedule in plenty of time for delivery, or be as realistic as possible with your editor when drawing up contracts. And, if you are a fiction writer, definitely think hard before accepting a two-book deal when you have not written the second book at all. Writing a second book under contract and to a deadline is a very different proposition from writing the first in your own time... You don't want to give a publisher any excuse to change their minds, after all.

Writers' top tip 37: Keep your editor in the loop

If you have any concerns about hitting your delivery deadline, let your editor know as soon as possible. They can help you and take measures to adjust the schedules. If you keep them in the dark and let the deadline pass, you put them and yourself in a difficult position.

Give yourself time

When you are self-publishing, it is a mistake to try to rush your book to market. No matter how legitimate the reason for such haste may appear, if you rush certain aspects of the publication process, then you will almost certainly regret it at your leisure once you receive the finished product. Here are the areas of the self-publishing process where you should definitely *not* cut corners:

EDITING

This is possibly the most important part of the publishing process. Quoting how long it will take you to finish writing your book without allowing time for proper editing is a big mistake. The editing process doesn't only pick up typos and grammatical errors; more importantly, it sharpens the reading experience and makes sure your book has a good structure, compelling voice, great pace and taut storyline. Whether you invest time and money to get an experienced book editor to work on your book or whether you plan to fulfil this function yourself, it is imperative that you allow enough time for this process. If you rush it, you will compromise the end product, and that will have a knock-on effect on the potential success of your title.

DESIGN AND PRINTING
Production quality is an important part of the process, yet it is the one area where would-be authors often feel they can cut corners. Asking a friend who is good at Photoshop or InDesign to do you a favour and create your book in his or her spare time is a false economy. The first impression created by your book is so important. If you are to persuade retail buyers, book reviewers and your readers to take your book seriously, then it needs to look and feel professionally produced. Make sure your designer and printer pay attention to detail and spend extra time on the cover – this is an area that often gives self-published books a bad name.

SALES, MARKETING AND PUBLICITY
Selling your books in to distributors, retail buyers such as bookstores or supermarkets, and on-line sellers takes time. Commercial publishers allow around six months for this process – as an individual newcomer, you should allow nearer double that. This gives you time to set up appointments to present to buyers and to get the title into the wholesale and retail systems. It also affords you the time to get a publicity campaign in place to coincide with the launch. And, if you are marketing and publicizing your book yourself, remember that book reviewers in the print media will need a review copy of your book at least four months in advance of their publication date.

Whether you are self-published or you have a deal with a commercial publisher, you can see that the route to publication is long and sometimes tortuous, and you need to allow yourself time for you and others to get the process right. In this way, you will produce the book of your dreams and do your writing justice.

Luck plays a part
As with all ventures in life, there is always an element of luck that plays its part when it comes to timing. You could do everything right in terms of meeting deadlines, having a

meaningful anniversary as a hook for publication, and leaving plenty of time for a spectacular marketing push, but sometimes the gods of publishing are against you. If your novel about Richard the Lionheart's brave deeds is published just as the headlines are full of reports of recent findings that show he was actually a despot who never lived in England, it will probably have an adverse effect on your sales. It's not something you could possibly have known about in advance; it's just bad luck.

Naturally, the inverse is true. Sometimes synchronicity can work in your favour. Perhaps the best example of perfect timing is that of Tom Wolfe's novel *The Bonfire of the Vanities*, which lampooned the hedonistic, materialistic world of Wall Street bankers and bond salesmen who referred to themselves as the 'Masters of the Universe'. It was published a matter of weeks after the stock market crash of 1987 known as Bloody Monday. In the wake of the collapse of the global markets and the ensuing recession, the book chimed perfectly with the public's recoil from the self-serving culture and unbridled greed of the 1980s. Luck was most definitely on Wolfe's side with the timing of his publication.

Focus points

✶ Allow plenty of time from delivery of copy to publication, as book production schedules are notoriously long-winded.

✶ Book fairs and literary festivals offer good opportunities for new authors to pick up advice and to network.

✶ Book proposals that are to coincide with forthcoming events should be pitched up to two years before the proposed publication date.

✶ It is worth familiarizing yourself with the best times of the year for publishing specific genres.

✶ If you are self-publishing, release the digital edition of your book at the same time as the print version.

✶ Avoid late delivery as it has serious implications. If you are experiencing delivery difficulties, communicate with your editor in good time.

✶ Do not be tempted to rush your book to market by cutting corners on some of the essential editing and production processes.

Next step

You have done everything within your power to avoid all the pitfalls of the writing and editing process. Now let's look at the ways to make sure you get your proposal right.

10

Getting your proposal right

In this chapter you will learn:

- ▶ *The elements of a good proposal*
- ▶ *How to write the perfect covering letter*
- ▶ *How to avoid the rudimentary errors that will get your proposal rejected out of hand.*

You may have thought the hard work was over once you had produced your manuscript, but there is a major task to complete before you can submit your book to potential publishers and agents – and that is to write a compelling proposal. From the submissions that I see, this is something that eludes many first-time writers.

If you are to stand any chance of acceptance, you must write a polished and persuasive proposal, and that requires an investment of time and concentration. The aim of your proposal is first and foremost to sell your book idea but, in the case of non-fiction, it is also to persuade the agent/publisher that you are the right person to write the book and that you have the necessary credentials (namely knowledge and experience) to do so. Otherwise, the principles of proposal writing for fiction and non-fiction are remarkable similar.

As he or she reads your proposal, the publisher wants to be able to satisfy him- or herself that:

▶ your book has something to offer readers

▶ your work is original and exciting

▶ there is a market for your book

▶ (if non-fiction) you are qualified to write it

▶ it is well placed within the competition

▶ it catches the Zeitgeist and is not too early or late.

It is your job to make sure you answer all these questions in your proposal and its covering letter.

Remember this: Never send original documents to a publisher or agent

Always have back-up files on your computer as well as on an online storage site or back-up pen drives/disks that you store in different places in your home, including a fireproof box, or even in a different location such as a friend's house.

The elements of a good proposal

Over the years I have written numerous proposals, many of which have been accepted while some have not. I have found that including the following elements, under these or your own headings, will cover all the details that a publisher or agent might expect to see. Keep your writing clear, concise and accurate – after all, they will be judging you not just on what you say but how you say it. And concision is the watchword here – many new writers go into far too much detail in their proposals.

▶ **Title page** This contains the title of your book, your name and your contact details.

▶ **Introduction** This should be four or five paragraphs long and is your chance to market your book idea to the publisher. This is where you include information on why the book is needed (some current statistics to back up your claims can be a good idea), what it covers and why people will buy it.

▶ **Target audience** Outline who is likely to buy the book and why it will appeal to them. If you think your book has international appeal, then say so here. And highlight any distinguishing features of your target audience that may interest a publisher from a sales/marketing perspective; for example, although the audience for a book on vintage Maserati cars may be small, readers are known to pay handsomely for books offering this rare specialist information.

▶ **Competition** You are required to point out what books of a similar ilk are already on the market. This does not necessarily have to be a negative. You only have to mention the most recent titles and then you can point out (subtly) that continued good sales figures for these books proves that there is a strong market for this subject, and that your book will appeal to this existing audience because it is written from a different angle, whatever that may be.

▶ **Marketing** You do not have to have amazing connections or a celebrity name, but it does help to show that you have thought about ways to reach the market or to get publicity for your book. This is the place to mention if you have a blog, newsletter, podcast or other social media with a following. Alternatively, do you give talks or run workshops on your specialist subject? All of these are what's known in the trade as a 'platform' and as such would be of interest to a potential publisher.

▶ If you have press or media contacts, again now is the time to mention them. But do not despair if you are without any of the above – it's not a deal-breaker. Simply leave this section out of your proposal as you don't need to draw attention to the fact.

▶ **About you, the author** This is where you can sell yourself to the publisher. It is not a CV, so do not include any information that is not relevant to how you are qualified or suitable to write the book. Include relevant background and credentials, brief outline of research you might have done, or experience that has a bearing on the book, as well as any previous publications. A publisher does not need to hear that your teacher spotted your writing talent when you were ten when you got a star for your essay – and then list every piece of writing since. Stick to the point. If you are an academic, resist the temptation to list your qualifications and papers unless they are directly relevant to the book proposal.

▶ **Chapter breakdown** List the chapter titles, followed by a brief explanation of what will be covered in each chapter. You are looking at one paragraph or possibly two at most per chapter. It is supposed to offer just enough information for the publisher or agent to see how the book will shape up.

▶ **Sample material** Together with your proposal, you should send some sample material. You need include only a couple of chapters from your book, and it does not have to be the first two. I recommend you send two strong chapters that are representative of the breadth of material included.

▶ **Covering letter** Your covering letter or query email is extremely important because it is this that will dictate whether or not a publisher or agent actually makes the effort to read your proposal. In fact, it's so important that I'm going to devote a whole section to it.

Remember this: Read the submission guidelines

Although I give general submission advice in this chapter, it is always wise to read the submission guidelines for a specific publisher or agent (if they have them). They are usually to be found on the company website. Make sure you follow them closely.

The covering letter

Your letter has to be tightly focused on the job in hand, which is getting the publisher or agent to read your proposal, so any extraneous information such as your academic achievements, the epiphany that led to you writing a book, or your hobbies should be omitted. You laugh, but you would be surprised how many authors include this sort of detail in their covering letters.

For a work of fiction, the following format is a good start:

1 Address your letter to a named editor.

2 A couple of sentences introducing the book, including title, word count and genre.

3 A longer paragraph or two in which you introduce the protagonists, themes, drama and premise of the book – enough to whet the appetite and capture the attention of the editor but without going into too much detail.

4 A concise paragraph revealing information about you and your credentials.

5 A final sign-off paragraph that wraps things up.

A non-fiction covering letter differs very little and may follow this sample template:

1 Address your letter to a named editor.

2 A couple of sentences introducing the book, including title, word count and genre.

3 A paragraph setting the scene for why now – perhaps some startling statistic, an innovative approach to a popular topic or a new revelation.

4 A paragraph briefly outlining the book's aim and content –
keep it brief!

5 A paragraph dedicated to your writing experience and/or
credentials – why you are the right person to write the book.
Be confident but not arrogant. Include any previous published
works and book sales, if they are suitably successful.

6 Concluding sign-off paragraph.

You can enclose a stamped, self-addressed envelope if you
require your sample pages to be returned to you, although I
cannot say with hand on heart that it is any guarantee they will
be sent back to you, as these things have a habit of slipping
through the net at a busy agency or publishing house.

Writers' top tip 38: Send your letter to a named person

Make sure you address your covering letter to the correct named person
in the agency or publishing house. It's worth investing some effort
in securing this name from the company website or talking to the
receptionist, as using the name of an editor who retired 18 months ago is
pretty much guaranteed to get you off on the wrong foot.

Submission howlers

Given the importance of your proposal and covering letter,
there are a few obvious blunders that agents see all the time and
which you should be at pains to avoid. The following is a fair
representation of the worst and most frequent howlers – you
have been warned.

▶ **Keep your letter to a page, or two pages at most.** Authors
who send three- or four-page covering letters simply do not
understand the workings of an agency or publishing house.

▶ **Grammatical blunders.** It jars on those who make their living
from the written word to receive covering letters, synopses
and sample chapters that are full of spelling, punctuation
and grammatical errors or that are badly written. This surely
stands to reason. So you must polish up your skills or make
sure you get your submission checked by someone who is
competent. I know I keep banging on about this, but if one

of the most common and excruciating errors such as 'its' for 'it's' and 'who's' for 'whose' crop up, then you are effectively vetoing your own chances of acceptance.

▶ **Comparing yourself to successful authors.** Editors and agents cringe when a new writer compares themselves to a great author or their work to some classic masterpiece. I often read manuscripts in the Mind, Body and Spirit genre and I am constantly amazed by how many new authors liken their writing to Paulo Coelho's *The Alchemist*. It always rings alarm bells. It is fine to suggest that your book is in the style of a specific author as that simply identifies the genre of novel, but that is as far as the comparison should stretch.

▶ **Self-aggrandizing.** This is very unattractive, so avoid the temptation to oversell either yourself or your book. Let the work speak for itself, and keep the information about yourself to a brisk couple of sentences – that ought to do it.

▶ **Talking your manuscript down.** Strangely, this is just as undesirable as overselling. It is a peculiarly British trait to apologize for something in advance, and you would be surprised how many potential authors do it, but you must have confidence and pride in your manuscript (just don't mention that you do).

▶ **Overestimating the market.** It is a temptation to overstate your potential audience but it is not worth it, as an experienced editor/agent will see straight through it. The same goes for estimating overseas sales, e-book audiences, movie potential and merchandizing opportunities – just leave these things to the experts.

▶ **Attention-grabbing gimmicks.** Wrapping your manuscript in tissue paper and tying it with ribbons, including gifts of chocolates or cuddly toys, substituting a photograph of an underwear model for your author photo (which isn't required anyway), coloured envelopes and paper, graphic messages – all these gimmicks have been tried, and none works. If anything, they simply annoy the editor, so play it straight.

▶ **Sensible packaging.** A standard self-sealing padded envelope is adequate. It does not need to be taped so securely that it is impossible to open on its arrival.

Your final checklist

Before you send off your proposal, get a friend to proofread it thoroughly and then go through it again yourself, double-checking for any of the common blunders mentioned above. Once you are confident that everything is ready, tick off the following checklist before sending your proposal on its way:

► Sample chapters and the proposal are typed, double-spaced, page-numbered and clearly printed on white paper using a standard font (such as Times New Roman, Georgia or Courier) in 12 point.

► Your name and contact details (including email and telephone number) appear clearly on the covering letter and the title page of your proposal.

► Your proposal and sample material are secured together either by a large elastic band or a large clip (no staples or ribbons).

► Your covering letter is single-spaced, and no more than a page long (two at the most).

► A stamped, self-addressed envelope (big enough to contain your package should it be rejected) is enclosed. This is optional, of course.

► You have paid for the correct postage for the package. If your proposal arrives in the publisher's post room with a demand for excess postage, it is unlikely to go any further.

Writers' top tip 39: Don't hold anything back

New fiction authors are often concerned that, if they give away the whole story in their synopsis, someone else will steal the idea. Occasionally, they hold back vital information with a breezy 'All will be revealed.' This is never a good idea. Too many novels have weak or illogical plot lines and endings, and the editor will want to make sure that yours does not. So don't hold anything back.

Case study: David Llewellyn, reader for Conville & Walsh Literary Agency

▶ On the covering letter

'It will, of course, vary from agent to agent and publisher to publisher, but all I require is a very short, carefully composed introductory letter that will accompany the submission. Too often, I receive covering letters that run to four or five pages and, without wishing to be seen as churlish, I just don't have the time to wade through a prospective author's life history, a list of his/her reading habits, career summary, etc. What I look for is a one- or two-line pitch or summary of the work, the genre it lies within, and information regarding other work, either published, unpublished or in progress. Prospective authors may claim that this doesn't allow them the opportunity to express themselves adequately, but my point is that the manuscript in hand is what counts, and I need to get to that as quickly as possible. The submission itself must be allowed time to speak for itself. Remember that I receive between 80 and 100 submissions each and every week. I do read and consider each one and try to respond within three working weeks.'

▶ On the synopsis

'I am looking for a one- to two-page synopsis. Many people find the synopsis a very difficult task to approach, and often I receive four or more pages, which is just too much. The synopsis is not meant to be a chapter-by-chapter summary. It should contain an overview of the submission, with main themes highlighted, principal characters described, physical and period setting. If it's a plot-driven novel, then outline any major plot developments, subplots, red herrings, etc. If it's a character-driven novel, then concentrate on character development, major events or decisions that impact on the characters' lives, moral dilemmas faced , and any psychological messages lying underneath. That's it really. Please, no promotional blurb, hyperbole or claims as to marketability or film potential. The agents and publishers will not need any advice on the commercial possibilities; after all, that is how they earn their crust.'

▶ On trying to stand out

'It's your writing that will make you stand out from the crowd. Enclosures such as Mars bars, Kit Kats and knitted mice (yes, I have two on my bookshelves) are very sweet, but will not affect my judgement. I often receive elaborately packed submissions, tied with fancy ribbons and decorated envelopes. Please, just keep it simple as such things give a very amateurish impression. Appreciate that this is a very hard-headed and professional milieu that you are trying to enter, so present yourself accordingly.

'For the same reasons, don't enclose photographs of yourself – this is not a beauty contest. Your work is what you are trying to sell, not an image of yourself.'

▶ On some cardinal errors

'There are some cardinal errors that appear across all genres of fiction. I receive an inordinate number of submissions that open with the protagonists waking up, rising from their bed, flinging back the curtains, motes of dust hovering in the early shafts of sunlight – I'm sure you get the picture. Proust started his opus in this fashion, but he was a bit of a one-off. There has to be another way to open a novel.

'A major cause of losing readers' interest is the habit of "telling", rather than "showing". Not an easy distinction to comprehend, but one that all authors must appreciate and strive to avoid.' (This major topic is covered in Chapter 7.)

▶ On first impressions

'The first half-dozen pages are so important. It is where you immediately have to establish your voice and your style and endeavour to both capture the interest of the reader and fire their imagination. As a professional reader, I respond very quickly to the strength of the writing in these early pages. We request 50 or so opening pages, so I then move through the submission to confirm that the writing is of a consistent standard throughout. If my first impression is good, then I will reread the whole 50 pages again, then refer to the synopsis to establish where the novel is heading. If that all seems to fit, I then compose a brief recommendation to the agents before forwarding it to them for their assessment. Everything is out of my hands from then on, as it is the agents who will make the ultimate decision about whether to ask for the whole manuscript to be forwarded for consideration. Their judgement about whether to offer representation will again depend largely on the quality and consistency of the writing, their own personal tastes and their extensive knowledge of the world of publishing.

'I cannot emphasize too much the need to get those opening pages right. I have had instances of poor opening pages that have been redeemed by a quality that emerges in subsequent pages, but don't tempt fate (or the reader's patience) by not giving of your very best in those opening pages. Study the openings of acclaimed and successful authors in your genre to gauge how they achieve a memorable impact.'

▶ On staying the course

'I have huge respect for any author who manages to put pen to paper (or a finger on the keyboard), and the agency for which I work has a reputation for actively considering and encouraging debut authors. Conville & Walsh has a very proactive approach towards emerging authors, with an outreach programme that entails the agents attending writers' workshops, writing groups and creative writing courses, and festivals the length and breadth of the UK, and even beyond.'

'Unfortunately, for the majority of submissions we receive, the prospective author will receive only a standard rejection letter. Limited staffing and time constraints preclude us from providing advice for most submissions, but we do encourage all authors to keep writing. It is a most satisfying and rewarding activity in itself, though, of course, getting published is the icing on the cake (oh, an example of an unfortunate cliché). Where possible, we do provide specific advice where we feel an author has identifiable and resolvable errors in their work, and, in these cases, we invite them to resubmit at a later stage.'

'The creative driving force involved in writing is formidable and, out of all the creative arts, I feel that fiction writing is one of the most demanding on the practitioner. On each and every page there has to be the balance between characterization, meaningful dialogue, scene setting, creating atmosphere, balancing "showing" and "telling", plot development, narrative pace and flow, while at the same time having an overall perspective on where everything is leading. Respect, as they say. For me, it's all a phenomenal example of what humans are capable of in a most positive way.'

'For those successful in attracting the attention of an agent, the process picks up pace once again. The author will be invited to meet and discuss his/her work; there will be first, second and maybe more drafts (a very rewarding thing in itself, the activity of self-editing); and then, when the manuscript has been finely honed, there begins the process of introducing the finished article around the publishing houses. The agent takes on this role, and you'll become involved again, once a receptive editor has been identified. A long and arduous road, and one which will require patience, commitment and a willingness to "stay the course". Good luck!'

Writers' top tip 40: Give just the bare bones of your plot

You don't have time or space in your proposal to go into all of the plot developments, so just include the major developments (three or four) that move the story along.

Try it now: Write a proposal/Do a pitch

If the thought of writing a proposal for your writing project fills you with dread, why not try writing a proposal for the latest book that you have read? It is good practice and somehow it seems easier to write about something that is not so close to your heart.

Another good way to focus the mind on what information to include in a proposal is to imagine that you are giving an 'elevator pitch' to the commissioning editor at your publisher of choice. Sit your partner or a friend down and tell them about your book and yourself. If you see their attention flagging, think about whether that particular piece of information was salient or whether you have taken too long to get to the exciting parts.

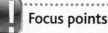

Focus points

✲ A concise and persuasive proposal is essential.

✲ Pay particular attention to your covering letter.

✲ Do not oversell or underplay the merits of your book – remain factual.

✲ Make sure your submission is laid out according to industry standards, includes all the relevant parts and is adequately (and not too securely) packaged.

Next step

To whom should you submit your proposal? In the next chapter, we look at the various and relative merits of agents and publishers.

11

Agents and publishers

In this chapter you will learn:

▶ *When to seek an agent*
▶ *When to go directly to a publisher*
▶ *What is the function of an agent and a publisher*
▶ *How to check a contract.*

Once you have a manuscript that you are proud of and you feel is marketable, you will want to find a route to publication. For many new writers, this can be the most fraught part of the whole process. Some writers go it alone when they would have been better advised to find an agent to represent them, and others waste time and effort submitting work to inappropriate agents and/or publishing houses. If you understand the role of an agent, and what a publisher is looking for, it will help you to make the best possible match for you and your manuscript.

What does an agent do?

A good agent will make your life much easier. They will guide you through the unfamiliar world of book publishing, using their experience and knowledge of the industry to find you the best-matched publisher possible and to get you the best deal possible. Having found a publisher, for, usually, 15 per cent of your earnings, they will negotiate your contract. This covers not only the book rights but those for audio books, digital editions, film rights and foreign sales – a minefield for the uninitiated.

Agents know the marketplace and will be able to advise on your proposal and on future projects – they have your best interests at heart because they have a vested interest in you and your work. An often unremarked advantage of having an agent is that they do all the wrangling and squabbling with the publisher over money, leaving your author–editor relationship unsullied.

Occasionally, if you have produced a highly desirable manuscript with obvious potential, a good agent will start a bidding war. This means that they effectively auction off your book to the highest bidder, and the interested publishers will raise their offers accordingly. This is a rare occurrence but by no means unheard of, and an experienced agent will know which publishers to pit against each other, and which is the best possible deal.

Where many new writers go wrong is that they believe an agent is there to fulfil the role of an editor, namely to improve your manuscript. If an agent takes you on, it stands to reason that they like your work – and they may well offer suggestions on ways to tighten up your manuscript, but that is not really part of their role. Nor is it their function to be your confidant and/or friend. Often that relationship develops over the passage of your career – I have been with my agent, Chelsey Fox of Fox & Howard Literary Agency, for over 25 years and I'm pleased to say that I count her as a close friend, but this is a happy by-product of a relationship that was initially purely professional.

Writers' top tip 41: Target an agent first

Don't send your manuscript to publishers and agents simultaneously. If you want an agent, target them first. An agent will be unimpressed if they take you on only to find that you have already approached various publishers – and very likely the wrong editor – and been rejected. This narrows the chances of getting a deal, as they cannot resubmit.

Do you need an agent?

This is a tricky question and one that, as an editor for The Writers' Workshop, I am asked all the time. The problem is there is no set answer. Certainly, if you are writing adult or children's fiction, popular non-fiction, a memoir, biography, travel book or popular science or history book, you would probably be wise to seek out an agent in the first instance. Why? Because most major publishers in these areas will not consider unsolicited manuscripts from an unagented author. If you go it alone, you are automatically reducing your chances of acceptance because you will have no access to a large section of the market.

However, if you are writing an academic book, a children's picture book or specialist or niche non-fiction, then you do not need an agent. For example, a book on eco-management and eco-auditing might well be snapped up by a legal publishing house without the need for an agent. Your book *Velocette Motorcycles from 1937 to 1962: The Golden Years* could get a motor publisher hot under the collar while *The A–Z of Crochet* might well ring the bell for certain craft publishers. These specialist publishers should be targeted directly.

Finding an agent

If you don't have a personal recommendation for an agent (always the best way in), then your first port of call when looking to find an agent in the UK is an up-to-date copy of *The Writers' & Artists' Yearbook* (A & C Black) or *The Writers' Handbook* (Palgrave Macmillan). (If you are writing for children or teenagers, consult the *Children's Writers' and Artists' Yearbook*). In the USA, agents are listed in the *Literary Marketplace*, the *Writer's Market* annual, and on writersmarket.com (a subscription website). The Association of Authors' Agents (AAA) in the UK and the Association of Authors' Representatives (AAR) in the US also have useful lists of names, and in the UK you can be reassured that the AAA's members have at least three years' experience and use a standard agreement letter with their authors. Contact details and web addresses can be found at the back of this book.

These directories and websites list all the agencies and any specialism they may have. You are looking for the best match for your manuscript and an agent who is not only going to be sympathetic to your work but who is knowledgeable in this area of the market. Clearly, you are not going to send your political thriller to an agent who deals only with non-fiction, nor is it advisable to send 'chick lit' to a publisher with a reputation for literary fiction. Apart from these obvious caveats, the field is wide open and agents are far more generic than you might think.

My own agency, which is a London-based literary agency, specializes in commercial non-fiction with a particular emphasis on biography, history, popular culture, reference, business, personal development, mind, body and spirit (MBS) and health. A pretty broad remit but, if their list were not full, they would in truth consider any non-fiction manuscript if they felt it was good and that there was a market for it. And the same goes for most other agencies. So don't be too hog-tied by apparent specializations.

So, keeping an open mind, scour the pages of the guides and make a list of those agents that chime with you and your manuscript. If you want to get further insight, you can always check out their website, although, in my experience, all are pretty slick and anodyne – they don't give much away about the true flavour of the agency.

Agents often give talks or participate in discussion panels at literary festivals, and this can give you a better insight into their modus operandi and whether or not they are a good fit for you.

Whether you look for one of the big-name, well-established agencies (where you will be one client among hundreds but they have reputation on their side) or a small one-man band (where you and the handful of fellow clients get plenty of attention but your agent has to do everything from opening the post to the accounts), there are advantages and disadvantages to your decision. Finally, it comes down to personal taste and instinct, but you may as well apply to a broad selection of older and newer, bigger and smaller agencies, and see what comes up.

Try it now: A sneaky way of finding possible agents

A sneaky way of finding the literary agency that might be right for you is to look at the acknowledgements in the front of a book by a new author who writes in a style that you like and favour yourself. New authors nearly always thank their new agents and editors; *voilà*. A little unorthodox, perhaps, but as good a way as any other of picking an agent to approach.

Pay a visit to a large bookstore or the library and pick out three books by first-time authors in your chosen field. Read their acknowledgements, and make a note of the agents' name and their agency. You now have three people to contact directly, but always take the precaution of ringing the agency switchboard to make sure that person still works there before addressing your covering letter to them.

Writers' top tip 42: Send your book in the best possible shape

Make sure your book is finished and in the best possible shape – perhaps a second or third draft – before you send it to an agent. If you send three well-worked sample chapters of a sparkling quality and the rest of the book does not live up to expectations, it can lead to understandable problems.

Remember this

A publisher is much more likely to consider a manuscript from an agent because they see them as a quality filter. If your manuscript has convinced an agent of its potential, then the publisher is more likely to take it seriously.

How to approach an agent

Once you have a list of, say, 10 to 15 prospective agents, your approach is the same as it would be to a publisher (see Chapter 10). Unlike publishers, it is acceptable to approach every agent on your list at the same time. In the happy event that more than one wants to take you on, you can then compare their styles directly and make up your mind. And if you only hear back from one agent, contact the others and let them know that you are now in discussions with an agent, which gives them the opportunity to give you an answer in good time.

Your submission should comprise a covering letter together with a synopsis and three sample chapters (usually the first chapter) and any introduction, if it is non-fiction. There is more detailed advice on what to include in your submission and covering letter and what to avoid from David Llewellyn, reader for Conville & Walsh Literary Agency, in Chapter 10.

Signing an agent's contract

The vast majority of agents now charge 15 per cent of your advance and of all subsequent earnings from direct sales, domestic and foreign, of your book and any digital versions. You should avoid any agent who wants to charge you to read a manuscript or for editorial services – most reputable agents offer this service for free, although, not unreasonably, they would expect a preliminary letter with synopsis and stamped addressed envelope to accompany your manuscript.

When you come to that wonderful moment when you agree that you are right for each other, the agent may want you to sign a contract. Rarely, a contract is only for the current book or project. More commonly, the contract is open-ended with a set notice period on either side (usually three months), although occasionally you may be asked to sign a time-limited contract, for example, a two-year contract that covers all work on your behalf during that period.

Make sure you read the contract carefully and, if there are any conditions or stipulations that you do not understand or that do not seem fair to you, ask about them or request that they are taken out of the contract before signature.

Naturally, during the tenure of the contract, you are not allowed to have your work represented by anyone else. However, if you move to a new agent, it is generally understood that if an agent sells a book to a publisher on your behalf, he or she will continue to represent you for that book and take their percentage for so doing, even if you are now with another agent.

Finding a publisher

If you have read these pages and decided that your work is better suited to being sent directly to publishers, then you must invest some time in finding the right publisher for you. Sending out your manuscript to publishers at random and with a scatter-gun approach is a sure-fire recipe for rejection. Although agents often accept a broad spectrum of writing genres, publishing houses (and editors within those organizations in particular) are remarkably specialist. Publishers receive hundreds of manuscripts and, if your book is not sent to the right editor or does not fit their profile, it will be rejected out of hand.

The key is to find a publisher who specializes in certain markets that dovetail with your subject area. Once again, you should consult the pages of the most current copy of *The Writers' & Artists' Yearbook* or the *Writers' Handbook*. Here you will find contact details for publishers as well as a round-up of their areas of expertise. Make a note of the best-match names but, before sending off your submission, double-check on their website or through the switchboard that your chosen person still works there and is still responsible for that subject area.

The other approach worth following is to look at books in the same general subject area at your local bookshop. Note down the publisher's name and address (found on the copyright page, which usually follows the title page) and then contact the organization to find out who is the best editor to approach for your subject.

Once you have a shortlist of publishers that specialize in the right area, you can prioritize which is the best option for you. You are aiming for a publisher that has books in this general subject area, perhaps from a different angle or related field, but not a book that is too close to your own.

Writers' top tip 43: Adapt your book to established series

If your book would sit very neatly into an established series that a publisher produces, it is worth modifying your manuscript so that it reflects that style. So this book is part of the Hodder Teach Yourself series. All the books within the series will have a similar writing style and will contain text boxes such as 'Remember this' or 'Try it now'. If you feel your book on *How to Master Underwater Photography* would sit happily on the list and there isn't a title on sale covering this topic at the moment, then it would make sense to modify your book with similar text boxes to fit the model, and so increase your chances of acceptance.

Another consideration is the size of the publishing house, although this is not always easy to spot as many of the large conglomerates have smaller imprints under their umbrella. There are advantages to being with a smaller specialist publisher, just as there are benefits to being with a larger organization, depending on your book, and it largely comes down to personal preference. Let's look at the pros and cons for each that you might like to consider.

SMALL PUBLISHERS
▶ Your book may get more attention if the company is producing only a few titles each year.

- Smaller teams can often make decisions more quickly and have more flexibility, enabling them to react more rapidly and make changes more readily.

- As a specialist publisher, they know their market inside out.

- You are less likely to get a large advance from a small publisher but your book may 'earn out' more quickly.

- Smaller companies probably have fewer resources for sales, marketing and distribution services.

- Smaller presses often look for new talent to nurture.

- Smaller publishers are often good for direct sales.

LARGE PUBLISHERS
- Large publishers have greater clout with booksellers, so can push for promotions such as the 'three for two' tables or shop-window presentations, and for bookstores to take higher numbers of copies.

- Advances tend to be higher from bigger companies.

- A recognized name can bring prestige to your book.

- Decisions take longer to be made and are harder to reverse or change in order to react to an unexpected opportunity.

- If you are a small fish in a big pond, your book may not get the promotion or attention it deserves.

You are now ready to make your submission. Unlike with agents, it is best to approach publishers one or two at a time – wait for a response and then you can send to the next name on the list, if you receive a rejection from your first choices.

Short cuts on to bestseller lists

In 2013 an investigation in the US discovered that some authors had managed to propel their books on to the bestseller list by unusual means. For around £46,000, a company called ResultSource (RSI) claims to be able to get writers to the top of the *Wall Street Journal* bestseller lists. (Scaling the heights of the *New York Times* list costs considerably more, apparently.) These prestigious lists actually have safeguards in place to prevent bulk orders skewing the list (the tactic used), but Forbes has revealed that RSI breaks bulk buys up 'into more organic-looking individual purchases' plus offers on websites such as Groupon. Since the investigation, Amazon has announced that it will no longer work with the company.

It is probable that this loophole will soon be closed but it just goes to prove that there are authors out there who are determined to make a name for themselves and their books by fair means or foul.

Writers' top tip 44: Watch out for 'vanity publishers'!

Bear in mind that publishers have no shortage of submissions through agents and unsolicited approaches from authors. They do not need to advertise. So, if you see a publisher asking for authors on the Internet, you should treat this with some suspicion, as it is probably either a self-publishing outfit or, worst-case scenario, a vanity publisher.

Case study: Liz Dean, Commissioning Editor for illustrated non-fiction books at Octopus Publishing

'I look for a really strong idea in a synopsis but it needs to have validation as well – so clearly define your concept and explain why you, the author, are the best person to write about this particular subject; is it because it's your trade, because it's a personal longing (something you've grown up with that you really want to express and explore, for example); or because your book has a historical hook that you feel is of value that has been neglected? Publishers can see whether an idea has got potential if they understand an author's burning passion for what he or she wants to write.

'If your synopsis is going to stand out, you have to be able to express the book idea in a couple of sentences, to be succinct, because, more often than not, the commissioning editor or publisher has to go and discuss that idea with just a couple of colleagues, or even a whole boardroom of people depending on the size of the company. And that group may include sales directors, marketing people, etc. who may not necessarily have an editorial background, but who need to get the idea in a nutshell.

'If the author can't explain the concept of the book in a couple of sentences, you can't expect the commissioning editor or publisher to then sell it to everyone else within the company, who then have to go out to bookshops and sell it, and so on. Understanding this chain of communication is helpful.

'Writers can do much to help themselves, such as researching a bit more about what a publisher does. Sometimes it's obvious you're getting multiple submissions and an author is just sending them out to everybody. Clearly, they've bought a copy of *The Writers' and Artists' Yearbook* and they've gone through it like a dose of salts. You need more mindfulness about what each publisher does, and show your awareness by including a covering letter or saying in your email, "I've noticed you publish these particular books. My book is kind of like your title *XX*, but it's unique because of these elements in my writing... and because of who I am." This gives the publisher a point of reference because the commissioning editor may be thinking, "Where does this fit in my list?" and not just, "This is a great book."

'Publishers are a lot more specialized than people outside the industry realize. There's a huge catalogue of books on offer from the big publishers, but they might have six to ten commissioning editors responsible for little chunks of that. So each commissioning editor is actually quite specialized in their field. If you're going to write to somebody, that's really good to know. Even if it's an exploratory email saying, "This is the subject I'm writing a book on. Is this something that you're usually interested in? Is this something you usually publish?" I think that would help to narrow down the submissions, so just submit to, say, three publishers that you've done some real research on. It's just a lot of wasted effort otherwise. If you're a good writer and you've researched your book, you should be able to research a publisher. That shows your skill and publishers really appreciate people who are dedicated.

'And, lastly, commissioning editors want to know what's new. If you have a particular interest and you sense a trend — it could be a new kind of crochet or a different type of meditation you have discovered — that you're excited about, it's worth putting forward. Bring something new to the table. Find a twist — something that makes it different. Publishers appreciate that.'

Remember this: Offer something fresh and original

Undoubtedly, it is hard for new authors to break into publishing, especially as business know-how points publishers towards established authors or young 'brands' such as celebrities and sportsmen and women. However, the fact remains that people within publishing, in the main, love books and are always looking for the next big name, so opportunities will always be there if you are offering something fresh, exciting and original.

Case study: Marcus Gipps, Editor, Gollancz/Orion Books

'As always, as with any editor, what I'm looking for are books that make me fall in love with them. We get so many submissions which are nearly there, which are competent and clever and well written, but don't have the spark that I need to be able to convince my colleagues, my bosses and our readers that this is something really worth investing in. I know that's a hugely unhelpful thing to say, and what one person loves another can be left cold by, but there it is. What it also means, though, is don't send us books with hundreds of typos, or with the "track changes" comments left on (this happens far more often than you would believe, often from very experienced agents), or saying "I know this needs a lot of work, but...". We get enough of that from the slush pile. Do be enthusiastic, please, as much as you like, but don't be unrealistic. Times are difficult; publishing is changing. We all know that, and sometimes our hands are tied.

'More generally (and usefully), Gollancz publishes fantasy, science fiction, horror, literary genre, some paranormal romance/urban fantasy and some YA crossover-genre stuff. Personally, I'm a fan of more literary stuff, but of course we're always on the lookout for commercial mainstream books as well. We don't see anything like enough hard SF, and it can sell really well when it works, so more of that would be great. The paranormal genre is declining here, although it's still strong in America, but we'll still take it seriously. It needs to be really good and different, though. We always like to buy world rights if we can.'

For more views on what fiction editors want, go to literary agent Andrew Lownie's website: www.andrewlownie.co.uk

Focus points

✱ An agent knows the industry, whom to approach and what is trending. They will get the best deal possible for you.

✱ Not all genres of book require an agent.

✱ Various annual guides and professional bodies publish lists of agents and publishers and their submission requirements.

✱ Choosing the size and age of a publisher comes down to personal preference, but it can be worth approaching various types in this regard.

✱ You can look for publishers with an established series and tailor your proposal to fit its format.

Next step

Some authors will experience the joy of having their book taken up by an agent or publisher. Many more will receive the inevitable rejection letters that are part of the publishing experience. We will examine ways to deal with such rejections and how to persevere in the next chapter.

12

Giving up too early

In this chapter you will learn:

- ► *How to cope with rejection letters*
- ► *How to stay inspired*
- ► *When to start the next project*
- ► *What it means to become a writer*
- ► *How to have fun.*

Your cherished manuscript, together with a well-crafted proposal, has been sent out to a selection of hand-picked agents/publishers and so the anxious wait begins. Many inexperienced writers imagine that a reply will be received within a few days from several of their choices, and in unguarded moments they even find themselves picturing a bidding war starting for their book. But what happens next, in reality?

In the vast majority of cases, you should brace yourself for bad news while hoping for the best, because, sadly, even if you have ticked all the right boxes and have a saleable book, there is no guarantee that you will get a publishing deal – at least, not on the first submission. And, in all likelihood, many agents/editors will not reply and the rest will be standard rejection letters, I am afraid to say.

Take heart, though, because there are many reasons why an agent or publisher may not take on your book. Perhaps it does not sit comfortably with the other titles or clients on their list, or it may be too close in nature to a book that is already doing well for them. Maybe the editor is not convinced that there is a market for the book or that the genre is as popular as you suggest. Or, possibly, it simply does not ring the bells of the editor who read it. That does not mean that it will not resonate with someone else.

Although it is undoubtedly painful to get a rejection letter, it is helpful if the editor or agent gives a reason for the rejection, as you can sometimes glean something useful from it. Then, if all correspondence is pointing to the same thing, then you would be well advised to take heed of the advice and make amendments to the manuscript.

Writers' top tip 45: Read the signs

If you have sent your proposal to half a dozen agents and all reject you, then it is probably fair to say that either there is something wrong with your manuscript or there is no market for your book. If, on the other hand, you are taken on by an agent and they fail to place your book, you can probably blame the market.

More often than not, however, you will simply receive a standard rejection slip with a terse 'No thank you' and no explanation. That is hard to take, but, paradoxically, the hardest rejection message of all to hear is that the editor or agent loved your book but is unable to take it on. Bitter-sweet rejection like that hurts even more, somehow. But take comfort in it because an encouraging rejection letter means that you are close to the mark and your book may well enjoy better success with another agency very soon.

Whichever the manner of rejection letter, you have to bear in mind that, just because one editor, reader or agent does not want your book, it does not mean that another will feel the same way. These decisions are subjective, sometimes arbitrary or, at best, based on criteria within the company that are beyond your control. Although it feels devastating when a rejection letter arrives, it does not mean that your book is a failure. Keep in the back of your mind the countless stories of bestselling authors such as George Orwell, J.K. Rowling, Stephen King and Zadie Smith who were all rejected, some countless times, before their eventual successes.

Remember this: Take rejection on the chin

Frequently, you will receive no reply at all to your submissions. Even a polite follow-up enquiry may not elicit an answer. While we all recognize that this is unforgivably rude, it is a reality that you must unhappily accept. Do not allow it to upset you or take it too personally – it happens to the best authors.

There is a halfway house between outright rejection and acceptance, and that is an invitation rejection letter. This is when an agent feels that your work has merit and that, if it were amended, it might be a saleable proposition and he or she would then like to represent you. In this instance, rather than let you slip through the net, you will receive a letter that has some recommendations for you to follow (possibly about the manuscript or possibly about adjustments for the market), and, if this is fulfilled to his or her satisfaction, a future collaboration is on the cards. Clearly, it is a matter for you to decide whether or not to make these changes, but the advice, especially about the market, is often sound and it might be the start of a future business association. A bird in the hand and all that jazz...

What to do next?

After a rejection, it can be a temptation to retreat into your cave to lick your wounds, vowing to write never again. This is not the answer. Of course, it is understandable that you feel disappointed and deflated but the best course of action is to already have another project on the go that is absorbing all your attention and enthusiasm.

Tempting though it might be, you should not abandon the original project. Depending on the feedback, you should send it out to another list of names, or make the suggested amendments to your manuscript and then resend it.

Meanwhile, console yourself with the thought that only people who are daring get rejected. Those who play it safe and never bare their souls in writing might not fail, but they will never enjoy the process or the possible success either.

If you are serious about writing, it is sad to say that you must develop a thick skin and learn to deal with rejection because it is an intrinsic part of the publishing process. Find what works for you, whether it be talking to sympathetic friends, a vigorous workout or solace in a few drinks, but work through it and get on with it. And I reiterate – do not take it personally (easier said than done, I know, but it remains true, nonetheless). Once you get to the point of being able to say 'Their loss!', then you are ready to resubmit and get on with the next project. Some published authors report that the desire to prove the critics wrong was the spur for them to carry on after receiving rejection letters. Better this than let rejection wear you down.

There are certain writing coaches who quote the adage 'Winners never quit and quitters never win.' I have to say that I do not subscribe to this theory when it comes to writing. Persistence is vital, but ultimately only you can know when you have had enough or when the constant rejections are taking too much of a toll.

Checkout Receipt

BISMARCK PUBLIC LIBRARY

Phone: 701-355-1480

www.bismarcklibrary.org

Hours: Mon-Thurs 9-9; Fri-Sat 9-6; Sun 1-6

PATRON: 23538000997025

How not to get published /
808.02 GIL 2013
39007002222156   Due: 04/30

_____

TOTAL: 1
03/31/18 11:33AM

So, should you give up? Well, if you honestly believe your book is publishable – and here you need to be brutally honest with yourself – then you will not forgive yourself until you have exhausted all possible avenues before quitting. Perhaps a different approach is required. If you have been submitting only to the bigger agencies, perhaps look at approaching a smaller agency or agent. Is your material more suited to a direct approach to a specialist publisher? Alternatively, you could consider new media as a viable alternative to traditional publishing (see Chapter 13).

For some, the realization that to get published often involves rejection or criticism of your work brings with it a re-evaluation of why they were writing in the first place. Perhaps you decide that it is the process of writing that appeals rather than having a book in the public domain. Or you may decide that print-on-demand publishing of a limited edition (so that you have books purely for a cherished few) is a better option. Sadly, for some, their hearts are no longer in it. In all of these cases, it may well be time to call quits on getting your book published via a traditional route.

Writers' top tip 46: Start a new project

As soon as you submit one writing project, start the next. Not only does it keep the creative juices flowing nicely but, if you receive a rejection, you can always reason that whether or not the rejected project eventually finds a publisher, this latest piece of writing is by far your best work to date. It is great for morale.

Try it now: Safeguard your ideas

Some new writers worry that an agent or publisher might steal their ideas. This is unlikely but not impossible. To safeguard yourself, keep a copy of all work and submission letters or emails that you send out. In the unlikely event that your work is plagiarized, you will be able to prove in court that you had the idea first. However, legal action is only worth pursuing if the thief has been successful, as you may then be able to entertain the idea of a handsome pay-out.

Staying inspired

If you have enjoyed the writing process, it can leave a big hole in your life when your book is finally finished. While you wait to hear back from an agent or publisher, it is a good idea to stay inspired by keeping your hand in with some personal writing or, as suggested above, to start on your next book. Or why not look at another genre of writing – a screenplay or a novella, perhaps? Even while you are persevering with submissions for your finished book, writing something new or researching one of your other ideas can be one of the best tonics for combating disappointment.

One of the biggest mistakes a new writer can make is to think that, having completed their first book, they have learned all there is to know about writing, arguing that they have ironed out problems and learned the tricks of the trade during the writing process. The one thing all professional writers will say is that everyone can benefit from input from other experienced writers and professionals who often see things that can help to finesse your style or give you inspiration. Good tutors will never try to change your unique style – another common misconception; rather, they will find ways to help you make the most of your idiosyncrasies and use them to best effect.

Here are a few ideas for ways to get feedback from fellow writers and professional coaches.

WRITING CLASSES

Joining a writing circle can be a good way to get feedback on your work from fellow writers. Naturally, you are also required to critique other people's work, but that, too, can be a useful exercise as it gives you insight into your own writing style. These groups are usually informal gatherings in each other's homes, although some larger groups hold meetings in schools and libraries. Newcomers are generally welcomed and you are usually given a couple of weeks to discover whether it offers the right approach for you.

The feedback should always be constructive and frank, but never discouraging or rude. In the vast majority of cases, writers' circles are supportive and productive environments in which to share your ideas and work.

Try it now: Join a writing group

Join a writing group and share your work, welcoming comments and feedback. But don't be shy – offer your opinion on people's writing as well. Your views are as valid as the next person's (even if they do have more experience) – reporting how a piece of work makes you, as the reader, feel can never be wrong.

Just one word of warning. Should you find that the group is dominated by the same voices each week, or if comments are unduly critical, it might be worth seeking out another circle.

RESIDENTIAL WRITING COURSES

Paying to attend a residential writing course might seem like a huge self-indulgence, but, in my experience as a course leader, spending time in the company of other writers, without distractions and with feedback from professional writers, really can help you to make great strides in your writing.

Again, there are probably more courses for creative writing on offer than for non-fiction writing, but courses specializing in certain areas of non-fiction such as life writing, journalism, creative non-fiction and scriptwriting do exist. And any advice on writing skills will never be wasted.

LITERARY FESTIVALS

These are becoming more and more common and they offer a great opportunity to meet your favourite authors in the flesh and to hear what they have to say about their work and the business. You can also participate in workshops and master-classes on a broad range of subjects, although early booking is advisable as they are always over-subscribed.

WRITERS' CONSULTANCY

There are a growing number of organizations that offer professional critiques of your work for a fee. The best use editors who are professional writers themselves and who know the industry and specific genres of writing very well. These established and reputable consultancies will commit to read your manuscript and to provide a comprehensive, candid and constructive feedback within a specific timeframe.

As an editor for Writers' Workshop, I recommend that you look at the testimonials of those who have used the services of a consultancy and check their conditions before parting with your money. You can expect to pay in the region of £250 to £350 for a comprehensive critique of a full manuscript.

MENTORING

One-to-one sessions with a mentor can be hugely beneficial to the novice writer, although these personal services can be expensive. Nonetheless, it is one of the most productive ways to develop your writing skills. You can find a mentor, like myself, through writers' consultancies – it is often an additional service they offer – or look online, but make sure that you check the terms and conditions as fees can become expensive if you are not careful.

Remember this: Getting professional support can be positive

As a writing course leader and editor for a professional critiquing service, I can say, hand on heart, that the vast majority of novice writers who use these services get something positive from the experience. Although not an impossibility, it can be hard-going when you write in a vacuum on your own. Getting the advice and support of professionals plus the fellowship of other novice writers that you meet on courses can help to sustain you and keep you inspired through your writing experiences.

Success and writing

Of course, we should not rule out the possibility that an agent or publisher will like your submission, ask to see the whole manuscript, and then take you on. Once your book has been published, you may decide that a writers' life is for you. And, as a professional writer, who am I to discourage you?

Nonetheless, there are certain considerations before you give up the salaried day job – and they are not all to do with remuneration, although that is a good place to start.

Those new to writing often think that it is a well-paid profession. Despite the few big-name authors who earn exceedingly large advances and royalties, most authors do not earn enough from writing alone to support themselves, so the vast majority write while maintaining a full- or part-time job. Even if you have signed your first book deal, you would have to be extremely lucky (not that it's impossible) to earn enough from the advance and royalties to take early retirement.

So, without wishing to sound unduly pessimistic, let us assume for now that you are writing in your spare time. Here are a few tips to prevent your cherished writing projects languishing in a drawer as the pressures of daily living take over:

▶ **Stay focused** It can be hard to keep yourself motivated, but always keep the goal of becoming a published author in mind, regularly reviewing your tactics for reaching that target, and continue to believe in yourself and what you are trying to achieve.

▶ **Have fun** You may decide that you want to keep your writing as a pleasurable but serious hobby and that getting something into print would be the icing on the cake; or perhaps writing a blockbuster may remain your lifelong ambition and nothing less will satisfy. Either way, you must remember to be enthusiastic, to take pleasure in the process, and to enjoy honing your skills so that you produce the best piece of writing for you, your reader and any potential publisher.

▶ **Choose your subject wisely** You have to have a passion for your chosen subject, whether it is fiction or non-fiction, as this translates on to the page. There is no good choosing a topic that you think might sell or appeal to a publisher if it is of no real interest to you – the writing will become a chore and a bore, and you will almost certainly abandon the project before the end.

▶ **Stay curious** The best quality of a writer is an enquiring mind and a curiosity about life. If you can keep this joyous trait alive and well fed by life's strange vagaries, then your writing will be all the better for it.

▶ **Keep inspired** Inspiration can be found in the strangest places. Whether you read a story in the newspaper and it gives you an idea for a new plot twist, or you hear something on the local news station that inspires a great idea, or through reading a jolly good book you get the impetus to approach your novel in a completely different way … inspiration is all around. If you keep your antennae tuned, you will be amazed at how it can feed into your writing projects and keep you on track.

Writers' top tip 47: Keep a handy notebook

Like many writers, I always keep a notebook in the car, as well as others dotted around the house – you never know when something interesting and inspiring is going to catch your eye. I even keep a notebook beside my bed so that I can jot down any ideas that come to me in the night as dreams, or in that half-awake, half-asleep state in the early morning when some of the best creative ideas are formed, but which are so easily forgotten later in the day.

Case study: Laura Wilkins, manager of Writers' Workshop, Britain's largest consultancy for new writers

'It's amazing how few aspiring authors seem to think, or even know, about editorial services. There is an understandable explosion of joy and enthusiasm when someone finishes the first draft of their first novel. It is undoubtedly an achievement and a display of commitment and focus. It might even be quite good, but rarely are such manuscripts actually ready to be sent out to agents or publishers.

'The point where the author feels that something is finished is exactly the moment at which they can mess up their chance of actually getting it published. Like anything else in life, knowledge is power and the worst thing one can do with their first draft is spend hundreds of pounds on printing and postage and whip a copy off to every address they can find in *The Writers' & Artists' Yearbook*. Before approaching agents, isn't it worth knowing what those agents are looking for? What they're hoping for? What they're expecting?

'Self-editing is, of course, important and, to some degree, an author might get away with conducting their own proofreading to ensure that the grammar and spelling are perfect. The two things an author really can't do is, firstly, approach their work with a truly critical eye and, secondly, have a real grasp of the demands of the industry.

'Even the most successful bestselling authors have editors and go through an editorial process long before the book gets published. Within the industry, editing is not seen as an option or a luxury; it's seen as an integral part of the process.

'Ideally, an editor works as the author's second brain. They understand what the author is trying to achieve and guides them towards that. This can be as intricate as suggesting rewordings of sentences or as broad as major plot developments or addressing issues of tone and style. The editor's job is to spot what's not working and help the author get the manuscript into as good a shape as possible on every level – technically, artistically and commercially.

'There is a misconception that an agent or publisher will be happy to read an unedited manuscript in its rawest form and be able to see the potential. Although, once you get a deal, you will be given an editor, the sad truth is that when the agent sees your manuscript, unless it reads exceptionally well, they won't be interested in it. This is a catch-22 situation. That's where companies like mine come in, providing editorial services to authors seeking representation.

'Our pool of editors come from an extremely wide background, representing every corner of the publishing industry. They're all published authors themselves but, more than this, they are experienced mentors and teachers with ongoing industry experience and highly tuned insight.

'The process of editing is both painless and rewarding. The editor reads your manuscript and then prepares a comprehensive report upon it. The reports are a bare minimum of 3,000 words long and they look at every aspect of the manuscript or screenplay. The rewrite that follows an editorial report is usually a transcendental experience. Unlike other rewrites, which usually feel like an unfocused act of just giving all of the elements a bit of a stir, a rewrite based upon an editorial report is like having been given the key to your own work: problems you hadn't noticed, simple solutions, nips, tucks and alterations – it all seems finally obvious and you're aware of your own work drastically improving.

'I'm not sure whether I hold with the commonly accepted knowledge that you get "one chance" with an agent, but I do know for a fact that every agent has an ever-growing slush pile of manuscripts and there's no point in putting your work in front of them if it's not going to be the best thing they pick up that week. They're certainly not going to look at the same manuscript twice unless they specifically request to.

'And there's the tragedy of the first-time author's absence of awareness about editing. After having put in all that time and energy on their manuscript, they miss the one step that would have given them a decent chance of impressing an agent.'

www.writersworkshop.co.uk

Focus points

* Rejection letters are painful to receive but you must not take them personally – they are an integral part of a writer's life.
* It is worth taking heed of consistent advice/criticism from agents/ publishers in rejection letters.
* It is not unusual to receive no reply to your submissions.
* Keep writing, and consider new genres – new ventures keep our writing skills fresh and polished.
* Use writing groups and professional writers' services to keep you inspired and to improve your manuscript.
* Enjoy the writing projects and stay curious.
* You could consider another route to publication.

Next step

Perhaps an agent or commercial publisher is not the right answer for your writing project. In the next chapter we look at alternative routes to publication such as self-publishing, digital books and print on demand.

13

New media and self-publishing

In this chapter you will learn:

▶ *How to publish an e-book*
▶ *The advantages of self-publishing*
▶ *How to gain a platform in and an entrée into traditional publishing*
▶ *Why you should write a blog.*

There are countless options available to authors now that just did not exist 20 years ago – self-publishing, print on demand, e-books, blogging and podcasts, to name but a few. Moreover, self-publishing has become respectable and is no longer sneered at by those in the books industry. Nor is it considered a last resort, as more and more authors, both new and established, now choose this option because, potentially, the rewards can be greater.

Whether you look at it as your first-choice route to publication or consider it only after receiving rejections from traditional publishers, there are still quite a few decisions that you need to consider before you commit to self-publishing, as well as some very common slip-ups that you would do well to avoid.

Remember this: Content is king

Sometimes the new innovations in technology threaten to blind us to one crucial fact, which is that technology may alter the way we consume media, but content is still king. Without good content, there is nothing to offer despite the dazzling new technology.

E-books

With the growing sophistication of mobile phones and the growing popularity of tablets such as the iPad and Kindle, there has been a boom in the number of e-books available. America led the charge, and in 2011 there were a whopping 35 e-book titles that had sales of more than 20,000, according to a *Publishers' Weekly* report. In the UK, sales of e-books are rising at an exponential rate, too – with no meaningful drop in sales of print editions, it would seem. According to the *Publishers Association's Statistics Yearbook*, the value of consumer e-book sales – including fiction, non-fiction and children's digital titles – was put at £92 million in 2011. That represents an increase in digital sales of 366 per cent, and this growth continued in 2012. However, to put that in perspective, e-books sales are still only the equivalent of 6 per cent of physical book sales by value, even though consumer print sales were down by about 7 per cent in 2011.

So why write an e-book? Well, for many techno-savvy young writers, it seems like an obvious choice. It is certainly easy enough to produce an e-book and you don't need expensive production standards as the differences between professionally published and e-published books disappear on black-and-white tablets. You can use publishing software to produce your e-book and you can then sell it through your own website by setting up a merchant account with your bank or by using a third-party merchant such as PayPal, which takes a small transaction fee.

Alternatively, you could approach an e-publisher – there are many to choose from. For example, with an e-publisher such as e-junkie.com, you pay from as little as $5 (£3.30) per month, for unlimited download bandwidth for e-books, although they have a 50MB storage limit. If you use a company such as PayPal or Google CheckOut to process the money and credit card order for your sales, you will end up earning about 90 per cent of the cover price of your e-book.

Given that you earn only about 10 per cent of the cover price if you have a commercial print publisher, you can see how many new authors feel that e-books are the future. And for existing authors who retain the digital rights to their print editions, this can be an attractive proposition, too. In 2011 J.K. Rowling started to self-publish, or rather she is producing her own digital versions of the Harry Potter books as she still owns the digital rights. They were never purchased by her original publisher – Bloomsbury in the UK – and they were never sold to any of her subsequent international publishers (including

Scholastic in the US). Rather cleverly, she is maintaining her relationship with Scholastic who will provide 'marketing and promotional support for the digital editions'.

And this is the nub of the problem. Marketing remains the crucial element in the success of e-books. As a new author, unless you can generate a huge amount of traffic to your website (and keep getting new visitors), you are not going to sell any books, and then you will be earning 90 per cent of nothing. So, the thing to bear in mind is that you must have a platform to reach a wide audience if an e-book is to be profitable for you, or if it is to reach the wider audience that you crave. Without a client base, platform or other route to the paying public, e-books are not going to make your fame or fortune.

When doing your costings and weighing up the pros and cons, you should also remember that e-books tend to sell for a fraction of the price of their traditional hardback equivalents.

What I would suggest is that you keep a close eye on this digital market as it is developing at an exceptional speed and more openings may become available very soon. The problems of marketing your e-book could be eliminated if the trend for mainstream publishers setting up digital-first imprints continues. Originally, this option was only available for genre titles – science fiction/fantasy, romance and so on – where the book was first released as an e-imprint and then released in print if it took off. However, in the States, Amazon and Penguin's Riverhead have published e-books in the field of literary fiction. Recently, Little, Brown UK launched Blackfriars, a digital-only imprint that focuses on new literary fiction and serious non-fiction. Watch this space.

Writers' top tip 48: Digital isn't a short cut to fame and fortune

Although there are now far greater openings for those wishing to reach a wide audience and make money from new media, including blogging, e-books and self-publishing, don't be fooled into thinking that this is a way to make a fast buck – to succeed requires dedication, investment and hard work.

Self-publishing

Many established authors who have a following of loyal readers are now opting to self-publish their latest books. But the big question is whether or not self-publishing is a viable option for the new author.

Unfortunately, there is no definitive answer to this question. Certainly, a lot of inexperienced and naive writers get their fingers burned by self-publishing because they believe the boasts of some unscrupulous self-publishing houses (even though there are good ones out there) who are shamelessly overambitious when it comes to estimating how many copies of their book they will sell. With more than 235,000 self-published books in America in 2012, the odds of writing a bestseller are slim. That doesn't mean it is not worth the effort.

For those with ready access to a paying audience, self-publishing can be a sensible and sometimes profitable decision. Or if, say, you have written the family history and you want some well-produced copies to give to family members to keep for posterity, then print on demand is a very good solution (see below). However, if you have no way to market your book or to reach your target audience after publication, self-publishing can be a costly business and you could lose every last dime that you invest in the venture.

Effectively, in self-publishing, you bear the costs up front or sometimes you are committed to buying a minimum number of books at a minimum price, and clearly you do not get paid an advance by a publisher.

The rather undesirable image of vanity publishing still taints self-publishing and so some of its members variously advertise their services as 'subsidy publishing', 'joint-venture publishing' or even 'co-contributing publishing partners'. The less scrupulous among them will ask for considerable amounts of money towards cost – contributions of £8,000 to £10,000 are not uncommon – and they will always give an unrealistically high prediction on sales figures. So you must be wary.

In reality, without an avenue to market, most self-published books will only manage to sell less than 50 books, and most of these are complimentary copies given out to family and friends. Occasionally, a self-published book will be a runaway success. In 2012 Amanda Hocking achieved eye-watering success with her self-published supernatural romances, and there were hundreds of thousands of readers for Hugh Howey's tale of life after the apocalypse, entitled *WOOL*.

The problem with self-publishing is that you can purchase various levels of services, from simple design to elaborate editing, but marketing and sales of your book are rarely part of the deal, unless you are prepared to pay considerably more. Nonetheless, if you have access to a large database, perhaps because you run workshops/courses/classes or because you have specialist knowledge and access to the associated specialist networks, then you can potentially sell a lot of books through these outlets yourself. And you stand to make a higher percentage of profit per book than if you were published by a commercial publisher. Otherwise, you would be well advised to factor in the costs of marketing and sales when you calculate how much your self-publishing venture might cost you. All too often, through my role as writing mentor, I see authors who are so caught up in the excitement of getting their opus into print that they do not give enough thought to how many copies they can realistically sell – and it is a costly lesson to learn.

On a brighter note, though, if you do achieve reasonable sales figures, you have something tangible with which to approach potential publishers, who may then be persuaded to take you on and to publish your book in the traditional way.

Try it now: Work out the worst-case scenario

Before you commit, calculate how much it will cost you if you do not sell a single copy of your self-published book. Hopefully that won't be the case, but is it a loss you could bear, in the worst-case scenario?

TYPES OF SELF-PUBLISHING SERVICE

As long as you are circumspect, you are actually spoiled for choice when it comes to self-publishing as there is a service to suit every pocket and all requirements. At the bottom end of the scale, there are companies who will print your manuscript in basic book form for as little as £70, and you then have a tangible expression of all your hard work: something to show for your efforts, even if it has not been published through a commercial publisher.

Going up the scale, you can choose from a full spectrum of services, ranging from the complete package – copyediting, structural editing, cover design, marketing blurb, etc. – to hand-tooled, leather-bound vellum volumes of great beauty. This top end of the market tends to be exclusively for treasured family histories or an ancestor's diary, for example, and, at up to £3,000 per book, it is not likely to be undertaken lightly.

A relatively new development is that there are now some publishers which are a hybrid between self-publishing and commercial publishing. Matador and Amolibros were at the forefront of this revolution, but other big names such as Simon & Schuster, Penguin USA and Hay House (Balboa Press) have also launched a self-publishing arm to their business. As the author, you still have to contribute some financial support but these new hybrid self-publishers draw on their commercial ties with wholesalers to get books marketed and sold. With this hybrid set-up, you might realistically hope to sell 250 or more copies of your book from a print run of, say, 500. Not bad going.

Try it now: Get your ISBN number

There is no point trying to sell your book until you have got an ISBN number and barcode, which need to be printed on the back cover of your book. Without these, no bookshop – physical or online – will be able to order your books. It takes about three weeks to acquire a number, with various payments required along the way, so research it now. Websites for the USA region and UK ISBN agencies can be found at the back of this book.

HOW TO CHOOSE WHICH PACKAGE IS RIGHT FOR YOU

There are three main reasons why people choose to self-publish. Some authors simply want to have their book in print – a lifelong ambition, if you like. Some use self-publishing as a marketing tool for their business, for example, if they are a leading specialist in their field or if they want to commemorate an important anniversary or event in their company's history. However, for the majority, the prime motivator is that they want to get their writing in front of readers, to get their message heard; and to be on the first rung of the writers' ladder, perhaps. Their reasoning is that, if a commercial publisher has not taken them on, then this is another way to reach an audience.

Once you have decided which of the above categories you fall into, this can help you to identify what you want to achieve from the self-publishing experience and, budget allowing, the option you should go for when choosing a self-publishing service. Clearly, if you are a hobbyist writer and you want a copy of your book as the culmination of your writing project, you are not going to want to spend vast amounts on the finished product. If it is for commercial clients and to impress your readership, then you will need to go for high production standards, which will have higher cost implications.

Writers' top tip 49: Cut to the chase

Do not set any store by the lavish praise heaped on your book and the high estimates of its saleability by self-publishing firms who stand to gain financially from your business. Rather, ask them the key question: what are their average sales per title published? And be persistent. Any bona fide self-publisher should be happy to answer this. And don't be shocked if it is around the 100-copy figure – this is at least realistic. If they continue to dance around the question and keep sidetracking you with salesman flannel, then you might be right to deem them untrustworthy and move on.

When deciding on your self-publishing package and provider, don't be afraid to search around and to compare services. Once you have established the crucial information in answer to the basic and first question, 'What are your average sales per title published?', then you can make further enquiries. Think along the lines of:

▶ How long have they been established? (Someone with a track record is useful.)

- How many titles do they produce each year?
- Do you like their approach?

Armed with all this information, you can make your choice.

SELLING YOUR BOOK

Once you have produced the best-quality book you can afford, you now have to sell it. And, as we have seen above, not only is this one of the hardest elements of the publishing process, it is often one that the author neglects.

You may have purchased a self-publishing package that incorporates marketing and sales. Even so, you cannot afford to be complacent. You have to be proactive to sell your book, either in conjunction with your publishing package or independently.

Your first priority is to get your book stocked in bookshops. If you get your book listed on Amazon as your first port of call, then at least you can direct all your customers there to shop and be sure that it is available and easy to acquire. After that, you can turn your attention to physical bookstores. You could contact book wholesalers or the co-ordinator who deals with independent publishers at large chains such as Waterstones and WHSmith, but be realistic in your expectations. You are competing with the big publishers, so acceptance in this arena would be a bonus. In the meantime, talk to local independent bookshops to see if they are willing to stock your book. Offer to do a signing – local authors are often popular with loyal customers.

And do not limit yourself to local bookstores – are there other venues that might be suitable? If you have written a steamy romance, perhaps the local beauty salons and hairdressers might be persuaded to stock your book by the till, especially if it has an attractive cover design. If the action for your crime thriller centres around the world of tennis, perhaps the local tennis clubs would stock it. Do not be frightened to offer a 'sale or return' deal – what have you got to lose? At least the books are out of your garage.

Market it through any networks you may belong to and use all your contacts and resources. If you run workshops, make sure it is available for sale at the venue. And, naturally, make it available for sale through or with a link to Amazon on your website, Facebook, Twitter and other social media accounts. Do not expect huge sales through these Internet avenues – unless you are prepared to market it very aggressively to a wide following – but every little helps.

Writers' top tip 50: Set a reasonable price

Do not be tempted to set the price for your self-published book too high in an attempt to recoup some of your costs more quickly, as this will only kill sales. The book has to be realistically priced against the competition and for the market that it is in. You may well be able to charge a high price for a niche subject-led book, but your recommended retail price (RRP) for a mass-market paperback needs to be competitive.

Print on demand (PoD)

This new digital technology now allows publishers to produce any number of books within a couple of days. This technological advent plays into the hands of the self-publishing author who only wants batches of books to sell at specific times and events. Say you have written a book on traction engines and you have taken a stall to sell spare parts at the country's biggest traction engine rally. You could print up 20 to 50 copies to take along and put on the stall alongside your wares.

One of the most popular PoD services is lulu.com, pioneered by Bob Young (who actually set up the Blooker Prize – see the section on blogging below). There are other PoD providers but all work in a fairly similar way. You upload your manuscript (suitably copy-edited) to the site and, when an order comes in, even if it is just for one copy, the PoD publisher prints the copy and sends it to you. There is usually a minimum price based on length and size of the book, and whether it is printed in black and white or colour.

Obviously, costs for the PoD service tend to be higher than self-publishing services where you print hundreds, if not thousands, of copies at a time. But, let's face it, you don't have to store all those unsold copies either, which has to be a bonus.

If you start with a PoD service and you find you have a good marketing outlet, or your book gets a good response, then you can either take it to a commercial publisher with its established sales figures, or you can go down the self-publishing route, ordering a few hundred, and continue to sell them yourself.

Just a final word of caution, if you go down the e-book, self-publishing or PoD route: I suggest you check the contract very carefully. In fact, I recommend that you get the contract checked out by the Society of Authors or a lawyer specializing in publishing contracts, as there can be clauses within it that might tie you in to royalty payments to the printing company. Also make sure that the contract specifies that the rights to your book and the files used to publish it remain with you.

Remember this: Don't cut corners

The biggest mistake made by new writers when it comes to producing a self-published book is that they cut corners when it comes to the cover and the design of the book. This is a false economy. A self-published book has to compete on an equal footing with commercially produced books when it is on the bookshelves, and a professional-looking cover is essential. You might have to pay a designer between £500 and £750 for this service, but it would be money well spent.

Are you blogging?

It is said that a new blog is launched every second. A blog is most commonly used as a kind of online diary. 'So how can that help me to get published?' you may be thinking. Well, there is a growing band of writers who are seeing a niche blog as a way to launch themselves as writers and to get their work known.

Clearly, this is a long shot, but it does occasionally happen. Blooks are books that are spawned by blogs, and there is even a Blooker Prize. Not convinced? Just consider chart-topping book and box-office hit film *Julie and Julia*, which started life as a blog by Julie Power, when she decided to document her attempts to work her way through all the recipes in Julia Child's 1961 recipe book.

In truth, it would be a mistake to write a blog solely with the hope that it will be picked up by an eager publisher and that you will receive a book deal. It is highly unlikely that this will happen. However, writing a blog for personal satisfaction and to practise the craft of writing is a good idea. And, if you get a following, who knows where it might lead? At the very least, you can promote your self-published book to your followers every chance you get.

Case study: Leila and Ali Dewji from Acorn Independent Press, self-publishing experts

'Since we started, two years ago, we have worked with a wide range of authors across different genres at different stages of their writing careers, who have arrived at the decision to self-publish for different reasons. The most common among these are: that they wanted to keep creative control and do things their way; that there is the potential to make more money as you keep a higher percentage of the selling price; that you retain all copyrights (make sure you're only granting a licence), and that the speed to market can be much quicker than the traditional model, when the time from when you first submit to a literary agent to the day you see your book published is usually about two years, or even longer.

'The publishing landscape has changed dramatically in the last few years. There has been a real shift in attitudes, mainly due to the vast increase in self-published authors and the quality of their work. Big-name authors such as J.K. Rowling and Jackie Collins are turning to self-publishing at the same time as publishers and literary agents are scouting the Kindle charts to pick up self-published authors.

'A huge sign of the times in terms of the attitude change is that many of the top UK literary agents such as David Higham, Lucas Alexander Whitely and Greene & Heaton (who have always made their money through traditional publishing deals) are now working with us to get their authors' work (both frontlist and backlist) to market and they see it as a viable and profitable option to generate revenue for their clients. This is not only when they have titles that they cannot sell to traditional publishers, but often because the deal put on the table by traditional publishers isn't as attractive as using high-quality self-publishing. Several literary agencies now have a member of staff responsible for self-publishing projects.

'Due to the gatekeeper-less nature of self-publishing, there are poor-quality books (both in terms of content and production) that make it to the market. While working at the literary agency, I did receive self-published books that were quite clearly first drafts and not ready for readers. However, it's up to the author to ensure that they work with a good editor, jacket designer and proofreader and that they do their research and look at samples from printers they intend to use. Also, if they are considering investing in marketing services, then they need to make sure they keep an eye on how often that company manages to get titles in promotions, secures press coverage, etc. We have developed strong* relationships with the merchandisers at the retailers, ensuing that we have titles in high-profile promotions every month, and employ specialist book PR agencies to build and implement our campaigns.

'Although attitudes are changing, at the other end of the self-publishing spectrum there are titles that haven't even been edited and have poorly designed jackets, which can prejudice people against them. Here is a list of the most common pitfalls of self-publishing paperbacks:

* Unprofessional content due to lack of editorial input – e.g. copyediting and proofreading
* Shoddy appearance inside and out – paper quality, binding, jacket design and typesetting
* Making poor and inexperienced decisions due to lack of professional advice and guidance
* Doing a huge initial print run
* Poor distribution – the most important thing for self-published authors looking to get stocked in bookshops is to get a distributor such as Gardners; otherwise, bookshops won't be able to order your book. Once you have secured a distributor, you will need to pitch your book to the booksellers and give them an advanced information sheet (like a press release with bibliographic data). Just like readers, bookshops make snap decisions on the blurb and the jacket, so make sure that this is as tight as possible. Selling your book in just one paragraph is a very difficult skill, so ask your editor to help you with this.

* Ineffective and inefficient (or lack of) marketing – marketing is a key part of the publishing process and is where many authors fall down. Even if you have a beautifully designed, well-written title available as both paperback and e-book via distributors and in the correct channels, your title is still one of thousands available, and, unless there is a proactive push to generate awareness, titles seldom succeed. The answer is to have a well-thought-out action plan that you can realistically put in place within your budget. There are lots of things you can do that just require your time and no financial input.
* Cutting corners – each component of the publishing process is as important as any other; there is no point having a wonderful story printed and bound on low-quality paper with an uninspiring jacket.
* Incorrect pricing – a self-published paperback can often have a much higher RRP than the books it will be competing with from trade publishers.

'Just producing an e-book can be a great option for someone just starting out, as the costs are lower. As above, you still need to make sure that the work is edited and thoroughly proofread. You do, however, need to think slightly differently about design – the image has to work at thumbnail size, as it will be displayed on retailer websites. Generally, this means that you want something simple and striking – lots of fussy detail will just get lost when the design is scaled down.

'Professional e-book production is essential if you want to ensure that your readers have a smooth reading experience on all devices – the last thing you want is bad reviews because there are technical errors in your e-book. There are a lot of companies out there who make it very cheap (and sometimes even free) to create an e-book through "meat-grinder" technology. This basically means that you input a file and the automated software spits out an e-book. However, the result is not always good and there normally is no way to edit the code (for example, to correct that one annoying paragraph that is right justified instead of left).

'With so many self-published books and e-books coming on to the market every single day, you need to ensure that yours is the best it can be and as professional as possible if you want to be able to compete.'

Focus points

✻ E-books are only available in digital format for tablet and smartphone users, but this is a rapidly expanding market.

✻ Self-publishing is no longer frowned upon and is a viable route to readers for many authors.

✻ You must be wary when selecting a self-publishing firm (rogues still abound) and choose with care which elements of their services are best for your book.

✻ To be successful, any book published via new media must have a route to its target audience, so you must have a promotion and marketing plan in place.

✻ New technology makes self-publishing and digital publishing easy for new authors but content is still king. Your book must be worth reading if it is to succeed.

✻ A blog can be a good marketing tool and very occasionally results in a publishing deal.

Further sources of information

UK guides for publishers and agents

Children's Writers' and Artists' Yearbook (A & C Black Publishers)

The Guardian Media Directory (Atlantic Books)

Willings Press Guide (Hollis Directories)

Writers' & Artists' Yearbook Guide to Getting Published (A & C Black) by Harry Bingham

The Writers' and Artists' Yearbook (A & C Black)

The Writers' Handbook (Palgrave Macmillan)

US guides for publishers and agents

LMP [Literary Market Place] (Information Today, Inc.)

The Writer's Market (Writers' Digest Books)

The Guide to Literary Agents (Writers' Digest Books)

The Children's Writer's & Illustrator's Market (Writers' Digest Books)

The Novel & Short Story Writer's Market (Writers' Digest Books)

Self-help and how-to books

GOOD WRITING

R.W. Burchfield, *Fowler's Modern English Usage*, 3rd revised edn (Oxford University Press, 2004)

Philip Gooden, *Who's Whose?: A No-nonsense Guide to Easily Confused Words* (A & C Black, 2007)

Martin Manser, *The Good Word Guide: The Fast Way to Correct English – Spelling, Punctuation, Grammar and Usage*, 7th revised edn (A & C Black, 2011)

Lynn Truss, *Eats, Shoots and Leaves* (Fourth Estate, 2009)

GETTING PUBLISHED

Claire Gillman, *Write Fantastic Non-Fiction and Get Published* (Hodder & Stoughton, 2012)

Stephen King, *On Writing: A Memoir of the Craft* (Hodder Paperbacks, 2012)

Stephen May, *Doing Creative Writing*, new edn (Routledge, 2007)

Dan Poynter, *The Self-publishing Manual: How to Write, Print and Sell Your Own Book* (Para Publishing, 2007)

Jason R. Rich, *Self-publishing for Dummies* (John Wiley & Sons, 2006)

Tom and Marilyn Ross, *The Complete Guide to Self-publishing*, 5th revised edn (Writer's Digest Books, 2011)

Aaron Shepard, *Aiming at Amazon: The New Business of Self-publishing* (Shepard Publications, 2009)

Magazines

UK

The Bookseller
www.thebookseller.com

Writers' Forum
www.writers-forum.com

Writers' News
www.writersnews.co.uk

Writing Magazine
www.writers-online.co.uk/Writing-Magazine

USA

Writers Digest
www.writersdigest.com

Writer Magazine
www.writermag.com

Websites

RESEARCH

American Library Association
www.ala.org

British Library
www.bl.uk
Tel: +44 (0)843 2081144

British Library Newspapers
Tel: +44 (0)843 2081144

Gorkana (UK & US)
www.gorkana.com

News4Media
www.news4media.com

Questia (online subscription library specializing in humanities
and social sciences)
www.questia.com

BLOGGING

www.wordpress.com

www.liveJournal.com

www.blogger.com

www.typepad.com

www.reporterswithoutborders.com (Handbook for Bloggers
and Cyber-Dissidents)

E-BOOKS

Adobe Acrobat
http://get.adobe.com/uk/reader/

Amazon (allows you to create a store front that accepts orders and processes credit card transactions)
http://webstore.amazon.com/

Directory of ePublishers
www.ebookcrossroads.com/epublishers.html

e-junkie (e-book publisher)
www.e-junkie.com

Google Checkout (processes online payments)
http://checkout.google.com/sell

Kagi (processes online payments)
www.kagi.com

Paypal (processes online payments)
www.paypal.com

SELF-PUBLISHING

www.acornselfpublishing.com

www.bookish.com

www.greenbay.co.uk/advice

www.troubador.co.uk/matador

PRINT ON DEMAND

www.antonyrowe.co.uk

www.grosvenorhousepublishing.co.uk

www.lulu.com

www.publishandbedamned.org

BOOK DISTRIBUTORS

www.bertrams.com

www.gardners.com

ISBN AGENCIES

Throughout the world, there are 160 ISBN agencies; each is responsible for assigning unique ISBNs to new books published within a specific region.

http://www.isbn.org/standards/home/index.asp handles the United States, the US Virgin Islands, Guam and Puerto Rico.

www.isbn.nielsenbookdata.co.uk handles UK submissions

Professional help for writers

American Press Association
www.americanpressassociation.com

The Arts Council England
www.artscouncil.org.uk

Association of Authors' Agents (UK)
www.agentsassoc.co.uk

Association of Authors' Representatives (USA)
www.aaronline.org

Author Network
www.author-network.com

The Authors' Guild USA
www.authorsguild.org

Authors' Licensing and Collecting Society (ALCS) (passes on photocopying and other fees to writers of magazine articles and books)
www.alcs.co.uk

Claire Gillman (writers' workshops and mentoring services)
www.clairegillman.com

GoldDust (writers' mentoring service)
www.gold-dust.org.uk

Jerwood Foundation
www.jerwoodcharitablefoundation.org

National Writers' Union (USA)
www.nwu.org

Online News Association (American digital journalism)
www.journalists.org

Press Association (UK)
www.pressassociation.com

Public Lending Right (PLR) (passes on fees from libraries to authors of books)
www.plr.com
www.plr.uk.com

Society of Authors
www.societyofauthors.net

The Writers' Guild of Great Britain
www.writersguild.org.uk

The Writers' Workshop (Britain's largest editorial consultancy for new writers)
www.writersworkshop.co.uk

Index